A year with Yours

Name	
Address	
Postcode	
Home phone	
Mobile phone	
Email	

In case of emergency, contact:

Name	
Telephone	

USEFUL CONTACTS

BANK	
BUILDING SOCIETY	
CHEMIST/PHARMACY	
CHIROPODIST	
COUNCIL	
CREDIT CARD EMERGENCY	
DENTIST	
DOCTOR	
ELECTRICIAN	
GARAGE	
HAIRDRESSER	
HOSPITAL	
LOCAL POLICE	
MILKMAN	
OPTICIAN	
PLUMBER	
SOLICITOR	
TAXI	
VET	

RENEWAL REMINDERS

	RENEWAL DATE	POLICY NUMBER	TELEPHONE
CAR INSURANCE			
CAR TAX			
MOT			
HOME INSURANCE			
TV LICENCE			
PET INSURANCE			
Yours SUBSCRIPTION			

THE YEAR AHEAD

Put a spring in

◆ Make the most of the increasingly lighter mornings by eating your breakfast by a window or even better, get out for a walk. A good dose of daylight first thing leads to better alertness in the day and improved sleep.

THE DAFFODIL CURE

Enjoying a beautiful bloom of flowers has long been proven to raise our spirits and make us feel happier. Studies show that patients in hospital who have flowers within view need less medication and can even recover faster than those who don't.

Meanwhile, floral scents have been shown to put us in a good mood and make us feel less anxious.

Daffodils are of course the star bloom at this time of year, famous for their cheering effects that scientists think could last for days. So fill your home with these golden beauties, or why not give a bunch of daffs to a friend in need of a lift?

your step

DECLUTTER YOUR MIND!

Spring cleaning may be a good way of freeing up some space in your home, but it can also free up your mind. Studies show a clear link between a clutter-free home and improved mood, sleep and ability to concentrate. The exercise involved in cleaning can also burn calories and help reduce the risk of illnesses such as heart disease.

If decluttering feels overwhelming, break it up into short bursts you can do for as little as ten minutes every day, perhaps starting with something as simple as organising your sock drawer.

EMBRACE APRIL SHOWERS

Instead of hiding from the rain clouds, head out with your umbrella to enjoy them. Rain produces a sound similar to white noise that helps calm our minds, while the distinct smell of rain known as 'petrichor' has a naturally relaxing effect.

Japanese researchers found walking in the rain could help speed up our metabolism as we burn more calories and build more muscle when exercising in cold, wet conditions, as you need to put in more energy than if you were on a non-slip surface.

For extra benefits, grab your wellies and jump in those puddles, as experts say tapping into your playful inner child in this way could increase your confidence and give you an uplifting sense of fun.

BABY LOVE

From ducklings to fluffy lambs taking their first wobbly steps, it's the season of new life, and taking as many opportunities as we can to enjoy it could do wonders for our mood.

Research suggests that seeing cute animals, whether in images, videos or in person, can reduce stress levels by up to 50 per cent, while reducing heart rate and blood pressure.

It's also thought that looking at baby animals in particular could increase our concentration, productivity and even our outlook on life – all the more reason to pay a visit to your nearest petting farm or watch cute animal videos on the internet.

HERDWICK SHEEP

Loved by author Beatrix Potter, Herdwick sheep are native to the Lake District. One of England's hardiest breeds, living on slopes and pastures, they can withstand the harshest of elements – even high up on the fells.

All Herdwicks are born with black faces, black legs and almost-black fleeces – a wonderful sight in spring. After the first year, their coats lighten to a dark brown colour and the wool on their heads grows out, revealing the white hair underneath.

Their heads and legs become white, and after the first shearing the fleece lightens further to grey, ranging from blue-grey to light grey. They are known as the gardeners of the Lake District, grazing on almost any kind of vegetation – from grass and heather, to bilberry, bracken, and young trees – and so have shaped the Lake District landscape as we know it today.

Springtime wildlife

NATTERJACK TOADS

The rare natterjack toad is found at just a few coastal locations in England and Scotland, in warm, shallow pools on sand dunes, heaths and marshes. Sadly, due to rising sea levels, just one or two colonies now remain in south-east England and East Anglia.

This special species is more olive-green in colour than the common toad and has a distinguishing yellow stripe running down its back. It also tends to run instead of walking or hopping, giving it the nickname 'the running toad'.

On warm, still nights in spring, the adult males gather around the breeding pools and emit a rasping call. The louder the call the more chance they have of attracting a female. Impressively, their calls can be heard up to a mile away.

GREAT CRESTED NEWTS

With its prominent wavy crest, spotted flanks and a striking orange belly, the great crested newt resembles a miniature dinosaur. Also known as the 'warty newt', it is the UK's biggest newt, and particularly fond of Norfolk's wetland habitats, as well as the central and south-east areas of the UK.

Adult great crested newts normally begin moving from their over-wintering land sites between February and April, with breeding taking place from around March to June. They undergo an elaborate courtship ritual, where males stand up on their front legs with their backs arched, waving their tails. After mating, each female lays around 200 eggs, individually laid and wrapped inside the leaves of pond plants.

Due to a massive decline in numbers, the great crested newt is now legally protected and is a priority species under the UK's biodiversity action plan. This means it is illegal to catch, possess or handle them without a licence, or to disturb their habitat in any way.

CAPERCAILLIE

A huge gamebird – the size of a turkey – the capercaillie resides in the native pinewoods of northern Scotland.

Males are mainly grey in colour and have reddish-brown wings with a white patch on the shoulder, hints of blue colouring on the head, neck and breast and red markings above the eyes.

Female capercaillie, in contrast, are much smaller with brown plumage. They can be seen all year round, but spring is the time to catch a glimpse of their flamboyant mating rituals.

This spectacle involves a series of click noises from the males, accompanied by a raised head, the puffing out of their 'beard' and their tail displayed like a fan.

Vibrant Oriental poppies

Words: Sarah Wilson

Does your garden need a quick and easy makeover to get it blooming? Plant these beautiful poppies now

When the big fat buds of oriental poppies burst open to reveal their colour-saturated, satin petals, it means summer is here at last. From crimson and apricot to saffron and cerise, often with velvety, jet-black splodges at their heart, these fantastic blooms come in the most sumptuous array of tones.

There are lots of different species, which means you can choose just the right height, colour and form to suit your garden style, but all have the signature floaty petals when they burst into flower. And they're a doddle to grow!

If you want to add a bold splash of red, you can't beat the exuberant 'Beauty of Livermere' (height 1.2m, spread 60cm, £5.99/9cm pot, crocus.co.uk). Tall and strong stemmed, they'll bloom through early summer and, although they tend to be quite short-lived, they make up for it, with each plant producing lots of flowers.

If you're loving the trend for dark-hued flowers, the rich, deep pink, tissue-like petals of 'Plum Pudding' (height 75cm, spread 60cm, £9.99/12 plug plants, thompson-morgan.com) bloom for longer than most oriental poppies, often from June through to August.

If you want to create a more ethereal look, there are endless pastel shades in the softest creams, pinks and peaches.

As well as an enticing mix of colours, there are all sorts of textures, too, with rumpled, crinkled and ruffled blooms aplenty. And, even after the blousy flower show is over, you'll have stunning seed heads to enjoy - leave them on and you'll have lots more poppies to enjoy next year, too.

PICK A HEALTHY PLANT

Widely available in supermarkets and garden centres, you can buy oriental poppies as potted plants, plug plants or loose roots. You can also sow them from seed. If you're buying a potted plant, look for plenty of healthy green foliage and sturdy stems. Avoid anything that is floppy!

When you bring the plant home, pop it in your conservatory or a sunny porch for two or three days, and gradually move it outside once there's no danger of frost.

KEEP IT ALIVE

Oriental poppies like a sunny spot with deep, fertile soil that's well-drained. So, if your soil is on the heavy side, dig in some horticultural grit (£2.99/5kg, crocus.co.uk) before you plant them.

HELP THEM THRIVE

Mix in some general-purpose fertiliser granules when you plant your poppies to get them off to the best start. You'll need to support them to protect them from the elements - just pop a sturdy support in when you plant. Although the seed pods are gorgeous, the plant will be stronger if you cut it back once it's finished flowering.

TOP TIP
While usually grown in the ground, oriental poppies are also happy in containers, and you can pack plenty in. Choose a deep pot as poppies have long roots, and use a mixture of John Innes No 3 (£3/10L, wilko.com) and a peat-free compost such as Sylvagrow Sustainable Growing Medium (£5.95/15L, sarahraven.com). Stand the container on pot feet as those roots will rot if they're too damp.

3 OF THE BEST FOR BOLD BORDERS

Perry's White
Features large, silken, pure white flowers with large, deep purple-to-black blotches in the centre.
£5.95/plant, farmergracy.co.uk

Coral Reef
An absolute stunner of a poppy, with pale coral papery blooms topping the strong, tall stems from late May to mid-summer.
£5.82/plant, ashridgetrees.co.uk

Carneum
An unusual soft-coloured variety with peachy salmon semi double blooms - very attractive and works well with silver foliage.
£3.99/plant, bosworthsonline.co.uk

Dress up your door

Breathe life into a neglected part of your garden with this stunning living wreath planted with hardy sempervivum alpine plants

MATERIALS:
Florists' plastic wreath ring base
Potting mix
Sempervivum (alpine) plants
Watering can
Hammer and a large nail
Pretty ribbon and garden wire

Seasonal craft

Gardening for Kids by Dawn Isaac, published by CICO Books (£14.99)
Photography © CICO Books

1 Drill holes every 10cm (4in) in the bottom of the wreath ring base and fill with potting mix to just below the top.

2 Take the plants out of their pots. If there are several sempervivums planted in one pot, then carefully break them up into individual plants.

3 Plant the largest first, making a hole for their roots with your finger and pressing the potting mix down firmly around them when planted.

4 Once the largest have been planted around the ring base, use the smallest plants to fill in all of the gaps in between them.

5 When the ring is covered with plants, water well and place on a flat, sunny surface outdoors. Keep the ring watered in dry weather until the roots have started to grow again and are holding the plants securely in the ring (this usually takes about 3-4 weeks). Hammer a sturdy nail into a door from which you can hang your living wreath, or suspend it using a pretty ribbon or a piece of garden wire.

Good day, sunshine

EAT AL FRESCO

Grab your picnic blanket and fire up that barbecue! Eating outdoors has been proven to have many benefits for our minds and bodies.

Being out in the sunshine showers us with mood and immunity-boosting Vitamin D, while being in nature, be it in our own back garden or at a local beauty spot, is proven to lower stress hormones and ease muscle tension. As there's lots to see, smell and hear outdoors, it's also thought al fresco dining increases our enjoyment of our food, encouraging us to savour every last bit. For extra benefits why not add some hand-picked wild blueberries, proven to help improve mental acuity as well as being packed with disease-fighting vitamins.

◆ Send an old-fashioned postcard this summer to a friend or a loved one, either from a place you've visited or just from your hometown. Handwriting notes has been shown to help foster a more positive outlook on life and is bound to brighten the day of the person receiving it.

Lift your mood...

BESIDE THE SEASIDE

From feeling the sand between our toes to gazing out at the wide blue sea, a trip to the beach can do us the world of good.

Researchers found even just a short beach walk can boost mental health and help tackle depression, while coastal locations have been found to be the happiest places on earth, even more so than green spaces. What's more, gazing at the sea alters our brain waves to put us into a mild meditative state... all the more reason to grab your walking boots and head off to the coast.

STALK THE SUNSET

Watching the sun go down on a long summer's evening isn't just a beautiful experience, it can also make us feel better.

Studies show people who feel connected to nature by taking a moment to notice the sunset report feeling happier and more satisfied with life. Research also found that when we experience this kind of awe - as it's hard not to do when the sky is on fire with colour - it can feel like time actually slows down, helping us relax and better manage stress.

GO ON AN ADVENTURE

Whether you set off on the summer holiday of a lifetime or simply go in search of a new walk or attraction locally, make the most of the sunnier weather to try new things.

Bringing novelty into your days, however big or small, has been shown to fire up new nerve cells. The more of these we produce the greater our energy levels, focus and general lust for life.

To get the most out of it, try taking up a new hobby or habit you can repeat regularly and with pleasure - from gardening to finding a new walking route every day. This builds new pathways in our brains which make our minds even more efficient and our mood more positive.

Summer wildlife

HUMMINGBIRD HAWK-MOTHS

With its long proboscis and hovering behaviour, accompanied by an audible humming noise, the hummingbird hawk-moth looks remarkably like a hummingbird while feeding on flowers. It has orange-brown hindwings which are evident in flight, greyish-brown forewings and a black and white chequered body. A summer visitor to the UK, it migrates from Southern Europe each year, but numbers vary. Some years, it can be commonly seen in gardens as it feeds on the nectar of honeysuckle, red valerian and other flowers. While you are out and about on a country walk, keep your eyes peeled for it along woodland edges, and on heathland and scrub.

ORCAS

Despite the name, a killer whale isn't a whale. Also known as an orca, it is actually a dolphin - the largest member of this family. It is one of the world's most powerful and intelligent predators, with the second-largest brain among ocean mammals.

The orca is easily recognised by its distinctive black and white colouring and gigantic dorsal fins, which can grow up to six feet high in males.

Scotland's west coast is home to the UK's only resident population - a group of just four males and four females - making a sighting rare, but not impossible.

Known as the 'west coast community' they arrive in Northern Scotland - particularly around the Shetland and Orkney isles - in early summer to feast on fish.

SAND LIZARDS

The sand lizard is one of the UK's rarest reptiles. It favours sandy heathland habitats and sand dunes and can be spotted basking in the sun on bare patches of sand.

It's quite a stocky creature, reaching up to 20cm in length. Both sexes have brown varied patterns down the back with two strong dorsal stripes. The male has extremely striking green flanks which are particularly bright during the breeding season in late April and May, making it easy to spot.

Sand lizards are confined to a few isolated areas in Dorset, Hampshire, Surrey and Merseyside as destruction of their habitat has reduced their range. Females lay their eggs in June and July burying them in sand exposed to the sun which helps to keep them warm. They hatch a couple of months later, just before going into hiberation.

SLOW WORMS

Despite its appearance, the slow worm is neither a worm nor a snake but a legless lizard. It is smaller than a snake, featuring smooth, golden-grey skin. Males are paler in colour and sometimes sport blue spots, while females are larger, with dark sides and a dark stripe down the back. They can be found across most of the UK, typically in heathland, tussocky grassland and the edges of woodland; places rife with invertebrates to gobble up.

If you have a mature garden or allotment - keep an eye out for them, as they are known to hunt around compost heaps. Like other reptiles, slow worms hibernate, usually from October to March, so the best time to see them is in summer when they can be spotted basking in the sun.

BUY NOW

Joyful petunias

Create a cheery splash of colour with a pot or basket packed with these fast-growing flowers

Like the loudest member of a band, the jubilant trumpets of petunia flowers herald the arrival of sunny months. They're a summer staple and while the bushy types look great in containers, there's been a recent surge in trailing varieties that's crowned them the kings of containers and hanging baskets.

If you want a hassle-free hanging basket, simply fill it with the Surfinia range of trailing petunias and you'll quickly have a cascading ball of blooms that's the envy of your neighbourhood. And while these pretty flowers won't last past autumn frosts, they're cheap as chips and will give you plenty of bang for your buck.

Ditch any ideas you may have that petunias don't have a place in a modern garden because, while there are plenty of old-fashioned varieties, there are lots of fabulously modern ones, too. Browse online and you'll be pleasantly surprised. From innocent all-whites to almost black, flowers with picotee edges (the rim is a different colour to the centre), huge-bloomed grandifloras and a mass of mini-petalled multifloras, there's a petunia that'll suit your plot perfectly. Start your search by looking up pictures of the colour-splashed 'Night Sky' – it's nothing short of outlandish! And don't be put off by people saying that petunias won't survive a wet summer, as the newer varieties have improved bad weather credentials.

PICK HEALTHY PLANTS

At this time of year, you can buy petunias as plug plants from garden centres, DIY stores, supermarkets and online suppliers. Select plants with lots of healthy, deep green leaves. Reject any showing signs of stress or damage, such as tired-looking yellowing, brown or wilted leaves. If you can, turn the plant upside down and ease it out of its pot – there should be a good mix of compost and roots, and not a tangle of pot-bound roots.

Words: Geoff Hodge

KEEP THEM ALIVE

Petunias prefer a warm, sunny spot, but can cope with partial shade. They love well-drained soil that holds plenty of moisture in summer, so dig in lots of bulky organic matter, such as planting compost or Verve Soil Improver (£4.37/50L, diy.com), and water in well. In containers, plant them in multi-purpose (£8/120L, wickes.co.uk) or potting compost (£1.50/8L, wilko.com).

HELP THEM THRIVE

To ensure masses of blooms all through summer, keep removing the fading flowers and ensure the soil or compost stays moist. Water thoroughly once a week or more often for those plants in containers - daily in the height of summer - and feed weekly using a high potash liquid plant feed, such as Phostrogen All Purpose Soluble Plant Food (£4.25/800g, homebase.co.uk).

HANGING BASKETS

Line your chosen basket with polythene and make a few holes in the bottom for drainage. Fill the basket with multi-purpose or potting compost, make small holes for each plant, pop them in and then firm the compost around them. Water in well. Try 'Purple Wave' (£12.99/24 plug plants, vanmeuwen.com).

3 OF THE BEST FOR BASKETS

Surfinia Trailing Mix
A prolific grower and available in a vast array of head-turning colours, these flowers are the staple of the British hanging basket.
Pack of six, £7.99, jparkers.co.uk

Petunia Star Mixed (maxi plugs)
Impressive rich raspberry, rose pink and deep blue petunias with a defined white star overlay.
Pack of 33, £9.99, jparkers.co.uk

Petunia Hippy Chick Violet
With its unusual flower shape and bright purple blooms, this showy new variety will add interest and colour to your baskets.
Pack of five, £5.99, thompson-morgan.com

Give your vases some va-va voom

MATERIALS:
Pages from a large book
(preferably with thick paper)
Ruler
Pencil
Craft knife
Cutting mat
Blunt knife for scoring
Craft glue

These sophisticated vase slipcovers give a beautiful sculptural form and are easy to make with a piece of paper and a few fancy folds!

Folded Book Art by Clare Youngs, published by CICO Books (£12.99) Photography by Jo Henderson © CICO Books

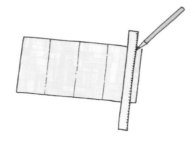

1 Using a craft knife (protect your work surface) cut a rectangle of paper from a page of your book measuring 30 x 14cm (12 x 5½in). On the reverse side of the rectangle (the side that will be inside the vase) mark a point every 7cm (2¾in) along the top edge. Repeat along the bottom edge and join the corresponding points with a vertical pencil line to divide the oblong into four equal parts with 2cm (¾in) spare at the end.

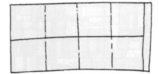

2 Draw a pencil line across the centre of the rectangle horizontally. You will now have made eight equal-size squares.

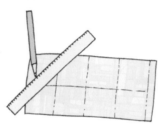

3 Starting with the top left-hand square, use a ruler to draw a diagonal pencil line from the bottom left-hand corner of the square to the top right-hand corner. Continue to draw an identical diagonal line in all eight squares.

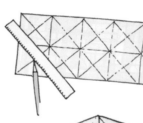

4 Return to the first square and use a ruler to draw a diagonal pencil line from the top left-hand corner of the square to the bottom right-hand corner. Repeat for all eight squares.

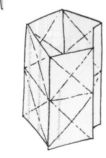

5 Score each of the four vertical lines and all of the diagonal lines. The only line not to score is the horizontal line running through the centre. Carefully fold the four vertical lines and then all the diagonal lines. As you bend the paper round to make the vase shape, the squares will start to form concave shapes with raised edges. Use your thumb and forefinger to ease the folds into shape by squeezing along the diagonal lines and gently pressing in the concave sections.

6 Spread glue along the flap edge of the vase and stick the two side edges together to complete the piece. You may need to reshape this section gently after gluing.

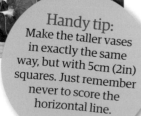

Handy tip: Make the taller vases in exactly the same way, but with 5cm (2in) squares. Just remember never to score the horizontal line.

Harvest happiness

KICK UP THE LEAVES

There's no better time of the year to embrace the calming power of British woodlands by crunching through the golden leaves.

Walking among trees is known to increase blood flow to the brain and release endorphins, the feel-good hormone that lowers stress and anxiety.

To take things one step further, try forest bathing, a Japanese concept that doesn't involve getting wet but means really taking your time to soak up all the sounds, smells and sights of the nature around you. It's thought to be so effective, some GPs now even prescribe forest bathing to patients.

HAVE A BREW

Warming up from the autumn chill with a nice steaming cuppa could be just the thing to help us feel good.

Researchers found drinking any kind of tea lowers levels of the stress hormone cortisol, but drinking even half a cup of green tea every day seems to lower the risk of developing depression and dementia. It's thought this is because tea contains antioxidants that have a calming effect, while also improving our memory and ability to focus.

Even just the ritual of preparing tea is said to have relaxing effects on the body. And drinking a cuppa after doing a stressful task can help you recover your composure more quickly. The soothing effects of a brew are even greater with chamomile which is a proven sleep aid as well as having antiviral properties - great for bolstering our immune system as we head into the winter.

◆ Going pumpkin picking? Don't forget to save some of the pumpkin seeds for an afternoon snack. Full of zinc and magnesium, they've been called Mother Nature's antidepressant for their mood-boosting abilities and are delicious sprinkled over yogurt and fruit.

HUNKER DOWN

Autumn is the time to enjoy a few home comforts including snuggling under a blanket with a good book or your favourite TV show. But did you know choosing a weighted blanket to wrap yourself in could have particular benefits for your mood and even help relieve pain and anxiety?

Weighted blankets work by mimicking a therapeutic technique called deep pressure stimulation, which has a calming effect that feels like a hug and can even help those who have trouble sleeping. They come in a range of different weights and materials and are available from some department stores and online.

AN APPLE A DAY

Whether you want to bake them in a delicious pie, join in with some seasonal bobbing or indulge in a little childhood nostalgia with the taste of a toffee apple, the apple season is great news for our mood.

After all, eating more fruit, including apples, has been linked to a much more positive mindset and energetic mood. It's also thought quercetin, one of the antioxidants found in apples, can help prevent cognitive decline while other studies show apples have been linked to a lower risk of heart disease. To get the very best benefits, eat the apples with the skins on.

WATER VOLES

Often mistaken for rats, the water vole has brown or black glossy fur, a blunt muzzle and small, black eyes. Unlike a rat, however, it has a chubby round-faced appearance, and its rounded ears are almost hidden.

Being a semi-aquatic rodent, water voles are found along rivers, streams and ditches, around ponds and lakes and reed banks, reedbeds and areas of wet moorland.

Autumn is a good time to spot water voles as the population is at its highest. They are most active during the day and will dive into the water when disturbed, making the familiar 'plop' sound. For signs of their presence, look for burrows in the riverbank, often with a nibbled 'lawn' of grass around the entrance.

Autumn wildlife

ROSE-RINGED PARAKEETS

The ring-necked, or rose-ringed, parakeet is the UK's only naturalised parrot. It is a large green bird, identifiable by its long tail, red beak and a pink and black ring around the face and neck.

Despite its tropical origins, the parakeet can cope with cold British winters - especially in suburban parks, orchards and large gardens where food is in abundance. It's thought that it became established in the UK in the Seventies, when captive birds escaped into the wild and began breeding. They are often found in noisy flocks in their hundreds - particularly in South East England.

Autumn is a great time to spot these birds - particularly in London's Richmond Park, where the season sees trees exploding into a kaleidoscope of colour.

BEAVERS

Extinct in Britain since the 16th Century, the beaver has now made a comeback after being reintroduced into the wild.

Europe's largest rodent, it can weigh as much as 30kg and measures well over a metre from head to tail. It has brown fur, a flat, broad tail and huge orange teeth.

It is among the world's best natural engineers, building dams that divert and slow running water, creating a mosaic of pools, marshes and wet woodland, which helps to improve conditions for other wildlife to thrive.

The young beavers, known as 'kits', are raised in a lodge, from which they emerge at the end of the summer. But the best time to see them feeding with their parents is autumn. Scotland's Knapdale Forest and the River Tay are said to be the only places in the UK with wild, free-ranging beavers. They can also be sighted in fenced reserves in England and Wales.

CHILLINGHAM CATTLE

Among the rarest animals on earth, these wild cattle are only found on the 330 acres of Chillingham Park, Northumberland. This is the sole surviving herd of a species that once roamed the forests of Britain. It is thought they have been living at the park for more than 700 years, despite being almost wiped out by the harsh winter of 1947.

Isolated from all other cattle, this historic herd is totally inbred yet remains fit and healthy – a unique situation without parallel in the natural world. You can see these beautiful white beasts up-close on a guided tour accompanied by a warden, where, if you're lucky, you can witness a battle between two ferocious bulls, fighting for the chance to mate a female.

This spectacle occurs thorough the year, but autumn is as good a time as any to witness it, when their fallow deer neighbours in the park begin their rutting season too.

Eye-popping Spindle Tree

Words: Geoff Hodge

Create a standout autumn show with glorious pink pods opening to reveal bright orange seeds inside

If you love autumn then you need a spindle tree in your outdoor space, as it is said to embody the breathtaking beauty of the season. Most are varieties of Euonymus europaeus, a British native, and you may have passed it by on summer walks, in hedges and forest edges. But come autumn, its spectacular riot of jaw-dropping, fiery colours will stop you in your tracks.

Its dark green leaves turn a blazing scarlet or buttery yellow but it's the fruit that steals the show. The summer clusters of small, yellow-green flowers explode into vivid pink, geometric shapes, the four lobes gradually peeling apart to reveal bright orange seeds inside. The crazy combination of colours is a real talking point, especially when autumn's low sunlight shines through the branches.

In the wild, this deciduous shrub grows to 3m high in 20 years, but you can tame it into a more compact size in your garden. Left to its own devices, it'll grow in a bushy shape, but you can easily remove lower branches in February so there's plenty of room for spring bulbs and summer blooms beneath. If space is tight, then Euonymus europaeus 'Red Cascade' is a good option, as it's more compact, growing out to 2m, and it has fabulously bright red autumnal leaf colours.

PICK A HEALTHY PLANT

Spindles should be available from many garden centres and nurseries, or buy from an online supplier. Choose a bushy plant with several strong, healthy stems for best results.

KEEP IT ALIVE

Improve your soil by digging in lots of planting compost or Verve Soil Improver (£4.37, diy.com). Although it will grow well in a lightly shaded position, for the most spectacular autumn leaf colours, position it in a spot that gets full sun.

HELP IT THRIVE

Feed your spindle tree in spring with a controlled-release fertiliser such as Miracle-Gro Rose & Shrub Continuous Release Plant Food (£6.50/1kg, homebase.co.uk). Mulch around its base with a thick layer of compost or bark in autumn or spring.

BERRY DELICIOUS

The Spindle tree isn't just an autumn treat for us, it's a reliable larder for garden birds including robins, blackbirds, song thrushes and tits. Robins will often defend it, making it part of their territory, and, interestingly, the tree is called 'robins' bread' in some parts of the UK.

Light up your living

Handy tip:
A lampshade kit
will include all you need
including lampshade rings,
self-adhesive lining panel,
double-sided tape and a
finishing tool. Alternatively
scour charity shops
for lampshades to
update.

Make this statement lampshade and create a cosy atmosphere with the help of a ready-to-use kit and an inexpensive fat quarter

room

Handy tip:
To help avoid creases you could wrap the fabric around a rolling pin and roll it out across the sticky sided lining.

MATERIALS:
1 long fat quarter 25 x 112cm (10 x 44in)
1 x 20cm (8in) lampshade kit
Sharp scissors
Iron and ironing board
Fabric spray glue and braid or fringing (optional)

Finished size will roughly be 20cm (8in) diameter x 19cm (7½in) tall

Fat Quarter: One-Piece Projects by Tina Barrett, GMC Publications (£12.99) available online and from all good bookshops

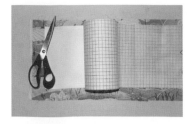

1 Lay out all your lampshade kit pieces. Iron your fabric and lay it out on a firm smooth surface with the wrong side uppermost. Peel off the backing from the roll of lining (from your kit) and smooth it out over the fabric, making sure the pattern is straight and avoiding creases. Using sharp scissors, trim all the edges close to the card.

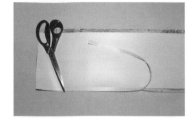

2 Snap back the plastic along the scored lines on the long sides of your lining, then peel off the backing.

3 Apply tape to the wrong side of one short edge and also to the outer edges of both round frames. Peel off the tape backing on both frames so the sticky sides are now outermost.

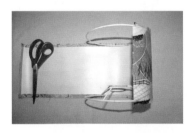

4 Line the round frames up with the long sticky edges of the shade and begin to roll the shade up. When you're near the end, peel off the backing from the tape you applied to the short edge and close the ends of the shade together firmly. Press along the seam several times to secure.

5 Using sharp scissors, snip down to the frame at the point of each spoke and tuck the bottom and top edges of fabric over.

6 Use the tool provided to push the edges around the metal frame. This gives it a nice rolled edge and a professional finish. Use fabric glue to apply braid or fringing to the outside edges now if preferred.

Winter comforts

FEED THE BIRDS

The chilly days mean British birdlife really appreciates our help at this time of year. But welcoming birds into our gardens by leaving out food won't just benefit our feathered friends.

Birdwatching can really help calm our minds, take us away from what's going on in our daily lives for a few moments and keep our brains healthy and active.

Watch out especially for robins, chaffinches and coal tits, all of which will be glad of some fresh unfrozen drinking water, a few fat balls and an 'untidy' area of your garden in which they can shelter.

◆ Staying out of the cold to settle down with a great book is a brilliant tonic for our mind. Studies show reading puts our brains into a state similar to meditation – and gives many of the same benefits. Reading just 20 pages a day has the power make us more empathetic, creative and rational too.

SCENT AND LIGHT

As the days are getting darker earlier, brighten up your evenings by lighting a candle or two. Candles have of course been used for centuries as a way of promoting calm; their gentle, mesmerising flicker helping make us feel more peaceful.

Scented candles have even greater benefits, with lemon, orange or vanilla associated with lifting our mood, while sandalwood and lavender help soothe. Adding candles to your home will also make it feel warmer and more welcoming, in keeping with the Danish idea of 'hygge' which is all about embracing the joy in the little things that make us feel comforted.

WHAT A YEAR

As the year comes to a close, it's a good time to look back and reflect on what's happened this year. Writing a journal is a great way to manage stress and express your feelings, helping you get in control of your emotions and improve your mental health.

If journaling doesn't suit you, how about making up a poem or short story about something you've felt or experienced this year? Creative writing can help us find a new perspective on ourselves, while studies have shown regular writing can lead to long-term happiness. Investing in some pretty stationery and setting aside a specific time for writing each day or week can really help motivate you into making it a regular habit.

BRING OUT THE BOARD GAMES

Whether you love Ludo or are mad about Monopoly, make the most of wet weather days by enjoying a good old-fashioned board game. Studies have found they help reduce stress and even the risk of developing dementia. As board games tend to be social, they also increase connections with the people we're playing with despite the arguments when the same person wins again and again! Be sure to involve the grandchildren as useful social skills can be taught through games that help build their confidence and happiness.

Winter wildlife

PINE MARTENS

It may look cute and cuddly, but with sharp teeth and claws and an appetite for small rodents, the pine marten is anything but!

A relative of the weasel, ferret and polecat, it is comparable in size to the average domestic cat. Its face is heart-shaped, with big brown eyes and a slim sinuous body. The rich brown coat turns darker in summer with a flamboyant apricot-coloured bib and long tail, bushy in winter.

The pine marten is notoriously difficult to spot but despite being less active in winter, a blanket of snow can make it easier to catch a glimpse of its chestnut-brown coat as it moves to lower ground for foraging during the colder months. If you fancy your chances, there are hides in Scotland and Wales for sighting these shy creatures.

Nature's wonders

HIGHLAND CATTLE

Eye-catching red hair, a trendy fringe and large curved horns – there's no denying Scotland's Highland cattle are a sight to behold. As well as shades of red, these gentle giants also come in yellow, brindle, dun, silver, white and black. Not only are their features very charming, but they also enable the cow to survive harsh winters while exposed to the elements – they're considered to be almost as cold tolerant as the arctic-dwelling caribou and reindeer. Their coat is made is of two layers, with an insulating thick woolly undercoat and an overcoat of recognisable long, straggly hair that sheds snow and rain away from their body. Even their long eyelashes and thick fringe of hair is designed to shield their eyes from rain, hail and cold winds. In the depths of winter, their big horns come in handy for raking away snow to reach grass underneath for grazing.

SCOTTISH WILDCATS

Stocky, muscular and rugged – the Scottish wildcat is certainly not to be mistaken for a domestic cat. On first glance, these felines may resemble a chunky moggy, but it actually has longer legs and a larger, flatter head with ears that stick out to the side.

Also known as the 'Highland tiger', it spends its time prowling woodland, hunting for prey such as rabbits and small rodents and maintaining its territorial scent markings.

As well as being extremely rare and elusive, it is also largely solitary but more sociable during the mating season in winter, which occurs from January to March. During this period males will search out females to mate with.

OTTERS

Whether it's just a glimpse of its long whiskers or beady black eyes, an encounter with an otter is a magical experience. It is adapted to life on both land and in water, with webbed feet for swimming and dense fur for warmth. An efficient swimmer, it can even close its ears and nose when fishing for prey underwater.

Although it is considered relatively rare, the species is widespread in the UK and exists in almost every country. For the best chance of sighting an otter, head to Scotland, the west coast of Wales, East Anglia or South-West England.

October to December is a particularly good time to catch a glimpse, when it frequents weirs and waterfalls to chase leaping salmon. As with all mammals, the trick to otter-spotting is patience, but dawn and dusk is when it is typically most active.

Dashing dogwood

Install an instant splash of colour with vibrant
stems that will brighten the greyest winter days

Winter gardens can look rather stark, so get shopping for a fast fix! The bare stems of dogwoods come in all sorts of exquisite colours. While reds are the most popular, there are yellow, multicoloured and black varieties available.

If yours is a minimalist modern garden, then the stems look gorgeous on their own, especially when backlit by low winter sunshine. Or if you like a more generous tangle of plants, then underplant with hellebores, daffodils and snowdrops.

Dogwoods also work brilliantly in large pots or other containers, so they make a glorious patio feature. Cornus alba 'Sibirica' is the best red with super-bright coral stems. Cornus sericea 'Flaviramea', commonly called the golden-twig dogwood, boasts yellow-green stems, while Cornus alba 'Kesselringii' has red-purple stems that turn almost black in winter. Try the pair together for an eye-popping contrast! Cornus sanguinea 'Midwinter Fire' is also a good choice with its fiery orange-red and yellow stems.

If you want more bang for your buck and variegated leaves, too, then Cornus alba 'Spaethii' sports bright red stems and leaves with bold yellow margins. The stem colour is always more vibrant on new growth – as the stems age, they lose their colour and eventually revert to brown.

Every March or April, cut back all the stems to around 5cm above ground level. It sounds drastic, but don't worry! They're fast growers and will soon grow lovely long stems again. If you want to keep some height and structure all year, then cut back half the stems one year and the other half the following year. This applies to all varieties except 'Midwinter Fire', which isn't as vigorous and should only be cut to around half its height.

Dogwoods are pretty fabulous for the rest of the year, too. Clusters of white flowers in May and June are followed by white or creamy-white berries in autumn and winter, and most put on a lovely show of brilliant yellow or dark red autumn leaf tints. The leaves cling to the stems for weeks, long after those of other plants have dropped away.

Words: Geoff Hodge

PICK A HEALTHY PLANT

Most varieties of dogwood are usually available from garden centres and nurseries, and you'll find a wider selection online. Choose plants with at least four to five strong-looking stems. Avoid those with thin, weak or brown stems and anything with dead growth at the ends.

KEEP IT ALIVE

Dogwood thrives in partial shade as well as sun, but the stem colour will be at its brightest in a sunny spot. It likes moist, rich soil, so dig in lots of compost or Verve Soil Improver (£4.37, diy.com) when planting.

HELP IT THRIVE

Water regularly in spring and summer to ensure the soil or compost doesn't dry out. Feed in spring and summer with a general fertiliser such as Growmore (£6.99/4kg, crocus.co.uk). And mulch around its base every year with a thick layer of any organic material.

TOP TIP
Plant near a pond or water feature and enjoy double the colour with rippling reflections.

3 OF THE BEST FOR COLOUR

Cornus alba 'Sibirica'
Its oval, dark green leaves produce small, creamy-white flowers in May and June. But it's really grown for the bright, coral-red stems that are revealed when the leaves fall.
2-litre pot, £16.99, crocus.co.uk

Cornus sericea 'Flaviramea'
Admire the clusters of white flowers that bloom in May and June and the oval, dark green leaves, which redden in autumn and fall to reveal bright, yellow-olive winter stems
2-litre pot, £16.99, crocus.co.uk

Cornus alba 'Kesselringii'
You'll love the small, creamy-white flowers in May and June and dark green leaves, which turn reddish-purple in autumn and fall to reveal dark-maroon stems.
2-litre pot, £16.99, crocus.co.uk

Winter berry and fir candle

This simple-to-make frosty-looking winter candle is the perfect way to welcome guests for a festive gathering...

1 Melt the stearin in the double boiler. Add the paraffin wax and melt to a temperature of 80°C / 180°F. Stir with a wooden spoon to disperse the wax. Cut small pieces of fir and small clusters of berries. Using the paintbrush, paint a little wax inside the vase and stick the fir and berries to the inside of the vase. Don't use too much, just a few dabs to hold the plants in place.

2 Put the smaller jar (or vase) inside the larger one. Pour wax carefully in between the two, making sure that it doesn't splash. Use a jug if your double boiler doesn't have a lip to pour from. Leave to cool.

3 When the wax is hard, very carefully pour hot water into the inner jar or vase and leave for a few seconds. This will melt the wax a little so that the jar or vase can be gently twisted and lifted out.

4 Cut a length of wick the height of the vase, plus about 5cm (2in). Fix the end of it into a wick sustainer using the pliers. Using a small piece of wax adhesive, fasten the wick sustainer to the inside bottom of the vase, scraping away any excess wax to stick it in place.

5 Cut a piece of wooden skewer so that it can rest across the rim of the vase. Tie the wick onto it with a loose knot. Check the temperature of the wax and heat up again if necessary to 180°F/80°C. Pour it into the vase up to the wax rim and leave to cool for about one hour.

6 The wax will dip, so heat the molten wax again in the double boiler and top up the candle so that the surface is level. Leave to cool completely. Next slide the skewer out of the knot and untie the wick, trimming it to about 2cm (¾in).

Materials:
Stearin
Paraffin wax
Fresh fir and berries
Thick glass vase
Smaller glass jar (or vase)
Wick
Wick sustainer
Wax adhesive

Handy tip:
Never heat wax directly over a flame or heat source. A bowl can be placed over a pan of water to melt wax, but a double boiler is safer and easier to use.

Tools:
Basic candle-making kit including double boiler, thermometer (up to 177°C/350°F), wooden spoon and jug
Paintbrush
Small pliers
Wooden skewer
Scissors

Handmade Candles & Smudge Sticks by Emma Hardy, published by CICO Books (£12.99) Photography by Debbie Patterson © CICO Books

Notable dates 2022

New Year's Day (Bank Holiday observed)	Monday January 3
Bank Holiday (Scotland)	Tuesday January 4
Epiphany	Thursday January 6
Burns' Night	Tuesday January 25
Chinese New Year (Tiger)	Tuesday February 1
Valentine's Day	Monday February 14
St David's Day	Tuesday March 1
Shrove Tuesday (Pancake Day)	Tuesday March 1
Ash Wednesday	Wednesday March 2
St Patrick's Day (Bank Holiday N. Ireland/Eire)	Thursday March 17
Mothering Sunday	Sunday March 27
British Summer Time begins (clocks go forward)	Sunday March 27
First Day of Ramadan (Islam)	Saturday April 2
Palm Sunday	Sunday April 10
Maundy Thursday	Thursday April 14
First Day of Passover (Jewish Holiday)	Friday April 15
Good Friday (Bank Holiday)	Friday April 15
Easter Sunday	Sunday April 17
Easter Monday (Bank Holiday)	Monday April 18
St George's Day	Saturday April 23
May Day (Early May Bank Holiday)	Monday May 2
Ascension Day	Thursday May 26
Spring Bank Holiday	Thursday June 2
Platinum Jubilee Bank Holiday	Friday June 3
Fathers' Day	Sunday June 19
Summer Solstice (Longest day)	Tuesday June 21
Armed Forces Day	Saturday June 25
American Independence Day	Monday July 4
Battle of the Boyne (Holiday N. Ireland)	Tuesday July 12
St Swithin's Day	Friday July 15
Islamic New Year	Friday July 29
Summer Bank Holiday (Scotland / Eire)	Monday August 1
Summer Bank Holiday	Monday August 29
Jewish New Year (Rosh Hashanah)	Sunday September 25
Trafalgar Day	Friday October 21
Diwali (Hindu Festival)	Monday October 24
British Summer Time ends (clocks go back)	Sunday October 30
Hallowe'en	Monday October 31
All Saints' Day	Tuesday November 1
Guy Fawkes' Night	Saturday November 5
Remembrance Sunday	Sunday November 13
First Sunday in Advent	Sunday November 27
St Andrew's Day	Wednesday November 30
Winter Solstice (Shortest day)	Wednesday December 21
Christmas Day	Sunday December 25
Boxing Day	Monday December 26
New Year's Eve/Hogmanay	Saturday December 31

THE YEAR AHEAD

26 SUNDAY

27 MONDAY

28 TUESDAY

29 WEDNESDAY

30 THURSDAY

31 FRIDAY

1 SATURDAY

Down memory lane

PLEASE LET IT SNOW!

I've always been a snow fan. When I was a child in the Forties and Fifties we had proper snow for weeks on end. Mum used to call me down for breakfast saying: "Jack Frost came in the night." I would get dressed in a hurry, wearing two pairs of socks inside my wellies.

There was plenty of fun going on in the school yard; children slipping and sliding, others having snowball fights. Nobody seemed to feel the cold! In the classroom we were greeted with a roaring fire. Our teacher used to put the crate of frozen milk in front of it to thaw out ready for us to drink at break time.

Dad worked shifts, but when he was able he used to meet me from school with a sledge that he had made for me to slide home on. Around the house, large icicles hung from the roof and we had to take care as sometimes they fell and injured people.

Before going to bed I liked to look out of the bedroom window to see the frozen landscape with the silvery moonlight making the snow sparkle like crushed diamonds.

Sheila Davies, Wrexham

Name that tune

Ever since we were 'just a little girl' we loved this hopeful song, performed by the original girl next door. Used in an Alfred Hitchcock thriller, it was later a TV theme tune.

A: Que Sera Sera, Doris Day

Word of the week

Eunoia

Meaning a feeling of goodwill or 'beautiful thinking', this wonderful word is the shortest that you'll find in the dictionary containing all five main vowels.

Try something new!

Volunteer in your local area. Make it a learning experience by picking an unfamiliar activity. To find out what's going on locally, visit the websites of Volunteering England (ncvo.org.uk), Volunteer Scotland (volunteerscotland. net) or Volunteering Wales (volunteering-wales.net).

Uncommon knowledge

Audrey Hepburn was paid a record-breaking salary to play Natasha Rostova in the 1956 adaptation of Tolstoy's War and Peace. $350,000 was the most an actress had ever been paid, and, upon learning this, Hepburn reportedly told her agent: "I'm not worth it. It's impossible. Please don't tell anyone."

Recipe of the week

THAI CRAB CAKES

SERVES: 4
PREP: 20 mins
COOK: 10 mins

600g (1lb 5oz) fresh white crab meat
(or frozen and defrosted)
1 red chilli, sliced
5 spring onions, chopped
2 garlic cloves, crushed
Handful of coriander
2 tsp Thai fish sauce
2 tbsp extra-light mayonnaise
Grated zest of 1 lime
1 tsp cornflour
Flour for dusting
Spray oil
Chopped coriander, to garnish

1 Blitz the crab meat, chilli, spring onions, garlic coriander, fish sauce, mayonnaise, lime zest and cornflour in a blender or food processor until well combined. Divide the mixture into 12 portions and shape into flattish round patties. Dust lightly with flour, then cover and chill in the fridge for 30 mins.
2 Lightly spray a non-stick frying pan with oil and cook the crab cakes, in batches, over a medium to high heat for 2–3 mins each side, until crisp and golden brown. Use a spatula to turn them carefully. Serve them hot immediately with a sprinkle of coriander.

one2onediet.com

2 SUNDAY

3 MONDAY

4 TUESDAY

5 WEDNESDAY

6 THURSDAY

7 FRIDAY

8 SATURDAY

Down memory lane

WE WERE THE CHAMPIONS

My parents, Gwen and Bill, ran The North Wales Hotel in the seaside town of Rhyl. The summer seasons were always busy with holidaymakers, but in the winter months the tourist trade was virtually non-existent so my father installed a full-size snooker table in the lounge in addition to the dartboard in the bar. I was delighted when I reached the age of 18 and was old enough to join the games' teams as well as helping my parents behind the bar.

Home games were always well supported, possibly as much due to the buffet supplied by my mother as our sporting prowess. However, our darts team had a surprisingly good year in 1962, winning runners-up cups in the singles and doubles competitions, and going on to win the Licensed Victuallers' championship shield in 1965.

The team photo, which appeared in our local newspaper, shows my mother holding the shield and my father, third from right in the back row, wearing his trademark cravat.
John Nicholls, Sedgefield

Name that tune

This 'ghostly' track from two virtuous siblings was going to be released as a B-side until DJs made it a hit, first in 1965 and then in the Nineties thanks to a film release.

A: Unchained Melody, The Righteous Brothers

Word of the week

Sploot

A relative newcomer, sploot was added to the Collins English Dictionary in 2021. If you're a dog owner you may already be accustomed to seeing your dog sploot, describing the position your pooch makes when they lie on their tummy stretching their legs out behind them.

Try something new!

Do an outdoors Pilates session. Take a smartphone, tablet or laptop, along with an exercise mat, and find a tutorial via YouTube. The Girl With The Pilates Mat channel - run by expert Rachel Lawrence - offers a great selection of videos for beginners and experienced alike.

Uncommon knowledge

When Gentlemen Prefer Blondes was taking longer to shoot than anticipated, Fox asked Howard Hawks how production could be sped up. He responded: "Three wonderful ideas: replace Marilyn, rewrite the script and make it shorter, and get a new director."

Recipe of the week

CARROT, GINGER & ORANGE SOUP

SERVES: 4
PREP: 10 mins
COOK: 15 mins
VEGAN

Good glug of olive oil
4 small onions, chopped
4 garlic cloves, chopped
2-3in piece of fresh ginger, finely grated
Zest and juice of 2 oranges
8 carrots, peeled and sliced
1 litre (1.8 pt) water with vegan stock or 4 tsp of vegetable bouillon
Couple of pinches of cayenne pepper or chilli powder (optional)
Sea salt and pepper to taste
To serve:
Coconut yogurt or vegan crème fraîche (optional)
Chopped coriander leaves

1 In a saucepan, gently cook the onion in the olive oil until softened.
2 Add the garlic, ginger and orange zest. Cook for a min or so and then add the carrots, stock, and cayenne pepper or chilli powder (if using).
3 Simmer until the carrots are tender.
4 Using a hand blender, blend the soup until smooth.
5 Add the orange juice and season with salt and pepper. Blend again briefly to mix.
6 Reheat gently. Serve with optional dollop of coconut yogurt or crème fraîche, and a sprinkle of chopped coriander on top.

vegetarianforlife.org.uk

9 SUNDAY

10 MONDAY

11 TUESDAY

12 WEDNESDAY

13 THURSDAY

14 FRIDAY

15 SATURDAY

Down memory lane

I TYPED FOR THE STARS

Working as a shorthand typist in a provincial hotel, I was occasionally asked to carry out secretarial duties for the guests, many of whom were well-known personalities. Rex Harrison dictated part of a script that needed altering for a play being performed locally while Peter Brough dictated a whole radio script for a Royal Command performance. I remember being glued to the radio to hear it being broadcast.

When the film Where No Vultures Fly was premiered in Newcastle-upon-Tyne, the celebrities attending included Dinah Sheridan, Anthony Steele and Van Johnson who hit the headlines by wearing bright red socks with his evening suit. Afterwards, we received a telegram from an actress asking if we had found her elephant hair bracelet. We didn't know what it might look like, but it turned out to resemble a piece of wire which one of the chambermaids had put away in the broom cupboard.

Among the pop stars who stayed at the hotel were Cliff Richard, who was very shy, and Tommy Steele who bounced with energy. Unfortunately, as an employee, I was not allowed to ask for autographs.
Pat Berkshire, Hexham

Name that tune

Originally titled 'Honey Pie' the flares and platform shoe-wearing band behind this track that sold nearly six million copies worldwide refused to be 'defeated' when they first played this song in a much-loved battle of music.

A: Waterloo, ABBA

Word of the week

Moonshot

This Sixties term originally described 'launching a spacecraft to the moon' but was used more recently by our very own Prime Minister. When discussing mass testing for Covid-19 in 2020, Boris Johnson used the word in the context of a 'plan that's so large it's almost impossible to achieve'.

Try something new!

Go forest bathing. This ancient Japanese process of relaxation involves moving through a wooded area slowly, taking long deep breaths and smelling what's around you. Research suggests that even as little as 15 minutes can help boost immunity and reduce anxiety. To find a nearby woodland, visit forestryengland.uk/search-forests

Uncommon knowledge

It's fair to say that Robert Mitchum wasn't really a traditional romantic. When he proposed to Dorothy Spence he said to her: "Stick with me, kid, and you'll be farting through silk". However, the couple were married from 1940 until his passing in 1997.

Recipe of the week

BAKED COD

SERVES: 4
PREP: 10 mins
COOK: 20 mins

4 cod fillets
30g (1½ oz) butter
2 onions, finely chopped
100g (4oz) fresh breadcrumbs
1 tbsp parsley, finely chopped
Zest of one lemon
1 tbsp freshly squeezed lemon juice
100g (4 oz) Opies Pickled Walnuts, chopped

1 Pre-heat oven to 180°C/Fan 160°C/Gas Mark 4.
2 Cut four squares of foil to wrap around each cod fillet and grease slightly.
3 Place one piece of cod on each square of foil and season with salt and pepper.
4 Melt butter in a frying pan and cook the onion until soft, stir in the breadcrumbs, parsley, lemon juice and walnuts.
5 Divide the mixture into four and place a portion on top of each cod steak.
6 Wrap foil loosely around the fish, place on a baking tray and bake for 20 mins.
opiesfoods.com

16 SUNDAY

17 MONDAY

18 TUESDAY

19 WEDNESDAY

20 THURSDAY

21 FRIDAY

22 SATURDAY

Down memory lane

OUR TREASURED CHEST

This beautiful oak chest which holds our precious family photos has a story attached to it. In 1916, my mother-in-law Ellen, aged fifteen, started work at Bourne & Hollingsworth department store in London. She lodged in the accommodation provided for the company's women workers in Gower Street and was befriended by Constance who was employed as a buyer.

As they became good friends, Constance took Ellen home to meet her family, including her brother, Donald. Her matchmaking was successful, love blossomed and their engagement was announced. Before she was to be wed in 1928, Ellen was summoned to Mr Hollingsworth's office on the top floor. As married women were not employed by the company, he presented her with a wedding gift of £5 and said: "There you are, Ellen. Now don't spend it all at once." But she did spend it all at once and bought this chest to hold her trousseau. It has been a treasured family possession ever since and among the photos stored inside it are ones of the couple who were married for more than 50 years.
Marie Papworth, Cheltenham

Name that tune

Almost cut from the film for which it is best known, this wickedly good song made a troubled star of its singer. It has been covered since by Eva Cassidy and Ariana Grande.

A: Over the Rainbow, Judy Garland

Word of the week

Run

With the most potential meanings of any word in the English language, 'run' has at least 645 different uses in the verb form alone. The word 'set' follows behind with 430 definitions.

Try something new!

Go stargazing! Download the Night Sky app, Sky Map app or Google Skymaps app to help identify the different constellations from your garden or backyard. Reduce light pollution by turning off indoor and outdoor lights (checking for hazards first), set your phone to night vision and point it up at the sky.

Uncommon knowledge

The director of The Awful Truth, Leo McCarey, had a very unique style, and liked to inspire spontaneity in his actors. He told Irene Dunne to answer the door with "Well, if it isn't my ex", and told Cary Grant to respond with whatever came to him, so the line, "The judge says this is my day to see the dog" was totally improvised.

Recipe of the week

THAI GREEN CHICKEN CURRY

SERVES: 2
PREP: 10 mins
COOK: 16 mins

80g (3oz) Thai fragrant rice (raw weight)
Low-calorie spray oil
200g (7oz) skinned chicken breast fillets, thinly sliced
1 tbsp green Thai curry paste
1 stick lemon grass, thinly sliced
2 garlic cloves, chopped
2 kaffir lime leaves (optional)
1 tsp Thai fish sauce
100ml (3½ fl oz) reduced-fat coconut milk
60g (2oz) mangetout, trimmed
60g (2oz) fine green beans, trimmed
Juice of ½ lime
2 tbsp chopped fresh coriander
1 fresh red chilli, shredded

1 Cook the rice according to instructions on the packet.
2 While the rice is cooking, lightly spray a wok or deep frying pan with oil. Place over a medium heat and add the chicken. Stir-fry briskly for 2-3 mins until sealed and golden.
3 Stir in the green curry paste and cook for 1 min. Add the lemon grass, garlic and lime leaves and stir-fry for 1 min.
4 Add the fish sauce, coconut milk and vegetables. Reduce the heat to a gentle simmer and cook for 10 mins, until the chicken is cooked through and the vegetables are just tender but still crisp.
5 Stir in the lime juice and chopped coriander and serve with the boiled rice, garnished with shredded chilli.
one2onediet.com

23 SUNDAY

24 MONDAY

25 TUESDAY

26 WEDNESDAY

27 THURSDAY

28 FRIDAY

29 SATURDAY

Down memory lane

BLESSED WITH FRIENDS

When my husband Eric died, I was in my 50s. Most scary of all, I had no close relatives - no children, brothers or sisters. But I need not have worried because my friends became my family.

As Eric was also my dance partner, I thought I'd never dance again as men who do ballroom and Latin at competition level are extremely rare. But now my friend Clare lends me her own life partner, Phil, and they put up with me tagging along in a threesome at dance classes. Theresa, my cousin by marriage, agreed to compete with me despite a busy life looking after her disabled husband, while my dancing friend, Christine, regularly shares coffee and counsels me by text.

There are many others; Nigel and Debs who include me in all their family occasions, neighbours Rachel and Steve who check that my blind goes up every morning, Rob who does all the heavy jobs I can't do with humour and kindness, and my London friend Linda who comes to stay for the weekend when we watch films together and treat ourselves to lunch in a swanky restaurant.

I can't tell you how lucky and blessed I feel.
Kat Crate, via email

Name that tune

We thought 'love was only true in fairytales' until we heard this upbeat song originally written by Neil Diamond. It was later introduced to a younger generation through the 2001 film Shrek.

A: I'm a Believer, The Monkees

Word of the week

Stiffrump

Some words do indeed sound exactly like their meaning and stiffrump is a great example. Sadly, no longer in use, a 'stiffrump' is slang for an obstinate or haughty person.

Try something new!

Join the **Yours** Book Club. Each month, we pick a book and discuss it in our welcoming Facebook group. With constant book chat, recommendations and a friendly community, it's a fun platform for discovering new reads and likeminded people. To join, visit facebook.com/groups/yoursbookclub

Uncommon knowledge

A sign of the times, when the first season of The Flintstones aired, it opened with an ad from its sponsor Winston cigarettes! This would later be replaced by the show's iconic theme Meet the Flintstones, first introduced in the third series.

Recipe of the week

TAGLIATELLE WITH BROCCOLI, THYME & MELTING CHEESE SAUCE

SERVES: 4
PREP: 5 mins
COOK: 10 mins

400g (14oz) dried tagliatelle pasta
200g (7oz) pack Tenderstem broccoli
250ml (½ pt) crème fraîche
200g (7oz) Tallegio cheese or brie, sliced
200g (7oz) Parmesan cheese, grated
2 cloves garlic, crushed
Small handful of chopped fresh thyme

1 Cook the tagliatelle according to packet instructions.
2 Meanwhile, cut the florets off the broccoli and slice the stems into chunks. Steam or boil for about 3 mins until tender.
3 While the pasta and broccoli are cooking, make the sauce by placing the crème fraîche, Tallegio (or brie) and Parmesan in a pan over a very low heat with the crushed garlic.
4 Add a small handful of chopped fresh thyme (oregano and marjoram would also work well) and heat everything gently, stirring to mix the melting cheese, adding a grind of fresh black pepper.
5 Once the sauce is ready pour it over the cooked pasta and broccoli and serve in deep bowls sprinkled with extra Parmesan and a good drizzle of extra-virgin olive oil.

Tenderstem.co.uk

30 SUNDAY

31 MONDAY

1 TUESDAY

2 WEDNESDAY

3 THURSDAY

4 FRIDAY

5 SATURDAY

Down memory lane

KEEPING TIME

For my 21st birthday my father presented me with a beautiful Accurist bark design watch plated in white gold. I was thrilled as this was the height of fashion at the time and very expensive. It had a tiny face which was hard to read even for my young eyes, but I didn't care because it was a stylish bracelet as much as a timepiece.

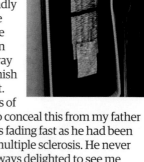

I wore it constantly, but sadly the plating on the reverse side of the elegant strap soon began to wear away which left a greenish mark on my wrist. So I cut thin strips of sticking plaster to conceal this from my father whose health was fading fast as he had been diagnosed with multiple sclerosis. He never knew and was always delighted to see me wearing it.

I am now in my 70s and still have the watch in its original box, complete with the ancient sticking plaster. Writing this has spurred me to take it to a jeweller's to see if they can resuscitate it so that I can wear my watch again, even if it's just as a bracelet.

Pauline Kenyon, via email

Name that tune

The writing sisters from Haworth, Yorkshire would have certainly been fans of this 1978 song that was written in just one sitting when its singer was 18. The accompanying dance moves are now legendary.

A: Wuthering Heights, Kate Bush

January 30 - February 5

Word of the week

Quarantine

The practice of quarantining started as far back as the 14th Century when the bubonic plague ravaged Europe. To try to stop the spread, ships arriving in Venice had to isolate on nearby islands for 'quaranta giorni' or 40 days.

Try something new!

Learn ten useful phrases in a new language. Use Google Translate to find words from your language of choice. Or download the Duolingo app - via Google Play or the App Store - for bite-sized lessons in Spanish, French, Chinese, Italian, German, English and more. Visit duolingo.com

Uncommon knowledge

When Julie Andrews was snubbed for the role of Eliza Doolittle in My Fair Lady, as she wasn't well known enough, Audrey Hepburn was brought in. Although Audrey did walk out when she discovered all her singing would be dubbed, she returned the next day and apologised for her "wicked behaviour".

Recipe of the week

ROASTED VEGETABLE BAKE

SERVES: 4
PREP: 10 mins
COOK: 30-35 mins

2 small red onions, sliced
1 large red pepper, deseeded and cut into chunks
150g (5oz) open cup mushrooms
2 courgettes, sliced
1 tbsp olive oil
Salt and pepper
6 large Lion quality eggs
3 tbsp chopped flat parsley

1 Pre-heat the oven to 200°C/Fan 180°C/Gas Mark 6. Put all the vegetables in a square baking tray or roasting tin, add the oil and salt and pepper and toss well to mix. Roast for 15-20 mins or until golden and tender.
2 Beat the eggs together until smooth. Stir the parsley and eggs into the vegetables and return to the oven for a further 10 mins or until the egg is set.
3 Leave to cool in the tin for 5 mins before cutting into wedges and serving warm with salad.

British Lion Eggs eggrecipes.co.uk

6 SUNDAY

7 MONDAY

8 TUESDAY

9 WEDNESDAY

10 THURSDAY

11 FRIDAY

12 SATURDAY

Down memory lane

LEARNING THE LINGO

My dad is Polish and settled in England after the war. This photo of me was taken when I went to Poland, aged seventeen, to stay with my aunt and uncle. I went for the adventure as well as to learn the language even though I'd never had any lessons. I thought I could learn by using my old-fashioned dictionary and Teach Yourself Polish for university students which described complicated grammar beyond my understanding.

To begin with I missed things like Mars bars, fish and chips, Jackie and Valentine magazines and English pop music. Once I burst into tears when I heard Cliff Richard singing The Day I Met Marie. Mostly I missed talking to my mum as there was no telephone, but everybody was very kind to me (although my mini skirts were considered odd). I made friends with two sisters who were still at school. Their teacher allowed me to join school trips for picnics in the forest.

Over the years, I have been back many times. Poland is a very modern country now and I'm always made welcome. And yes, I did eventually become fluent in the language.
Krystyna Beech, Newton Abbot

Name that tune

Whether you're a brother or a mum, you'll have disco-danced to this iconic track. It accompanied the strut of a well-loved movie star and is now used to guide the pace of CPR.

A: Stayin' Alive', the Bee Gees

Word of the week

Shambles

Shambles began life meaning stool, then a meat table, before becoming a word for a slaughterhouse. In Shakespeare's Othello and Charlotte Bronte's Jane Eyre it still has this rather gruesome meaning, but today, just like its history, it just means a right old mess!

Try something new!

Sketch a familiar view. Grab a notebook and pencil and pick a point of interest in your local area - be it a historic building, local shop or a riverside view. Better still, find somewhere at home, like your favourite view from a window or a pretty spot in the garden.

Uncommon knowledge

The film that made Marlon Brando a star, Tennessee Williams' A Streetcar Named Desire (1951) was met with critical praise. Jessica Tandy was the only member of its original Broadway cast to not reprise her role in the film, Warner Brothers wanted a big name to fill the part of Blanche DuBois and went with Vivien Leigh, who'd played the part on London's West End.

Recipe of the week

SAUSAGE & RATATOUILLE CASSEROLE

SERVES: 4
PREP: 5 mins
COOK: 20 mins

8 pork sausages
400g (1lb 2oz) tin of new potatoes, diced
400g (1lb 2oz) tin of chopped tomatoes
390g (1lb 2oz) tin of ratatouille
Handful of chopped parsley

1 Place the sausages under a pre-heated grill for 15 mins, turning occasionally. Cut into thick slices once cooked.
2 Meanwhile, cook the potatoes in boiling water for 10 mins until tender, drain and return to the pan, add the tomatoes and ratatouille and simmer for 5 mins.
3 Stir in the sausages and cook for 2-3 mins. Sprinkle over the parsley and serve.

Waitrose.com

13 SUNDAY

14 MONDAY

15 TUESDAY

16 WEDNESDAY

17 THURSDAY

18 FRIDAY

19 SATURDAY

Down memory lane

WORKING NINE TO FIVE

Now that I'm retired I do voluntary work, but I have had many jobs in my lifetime, starting with helping my older brother deliver newspapers. When my friend and I went to the local speedway, I saw raffle tickets being sold and thought 'I can do that' so we were soon earning money plus free entrance to the venue every week. I also had a Saturday job in a newsagent, earning 15 shillings a week while my friends in Woolworth's were only paid 12s 6d.

Later I had a well-paid office job, but there was always the lure of earning money to pay for a holiday or driving lessons. On a date one evening, I noticed that the girls serving behind the pub bar seemed to be enjoying chatting with the customers. Again, I thought 'I can do that' and the next week I joined them. I still have friends from those enjoyable times.

When I was made redundant from my office job I became a security officer working on cruise ships for several years. In between times I found work in department stores over the Christmas period as well as being an Avon lady.
Christine Young, via email

Name that tune

This 1987 single was certainly not a train wreck for the pocket rocket that performed it. In fact, it stayed at Australia's No 1 for seven weeks following an impromptu performance at an Oz football charity event.

A: Locomotion, Kylie Minogue

Word of the week

Smicker

Ogling, but in an appreciative way. In its Scottish verb meaning, to 'smicker' is to look at someone amorously. As an English verb, smicker is less intense, meaning beautiful, pretty or handsome.

Try something new!

Be a tourist in your town or city. Visit all the popular sites you've never been to. Use Google Maps to check their location and write a list before setting off. If you know your local area too well, take the bus to a nearby village you've never visited before.

Uncommon knowledge

The Bishop's Wife was selected for 1947's Royal Command Film Performance with Queen Elizabeth II and Princess Margaret in attendance. David Niven remarked: "The Queen and Princess Margaret told me afterwards and at great length how much they had enjoyed it."

Recipe of the week

INDIAN OMELETTE

SERVES: 4
PREP: 15 mins
COOK: 12 mins

Olive oil
8 large British Lion eggs
1 onion, chopped
1 green chilli, deseeded and chopped
4 tomatoes, chopped
1 tbsp garam masala
1 tbsp curry powder
2 tsp cumin
Salt to season
Coriander, chopped, to garnish

1 Heat the oil in a non-stick frying pan, add the onion and fry for 4 mins until soft. Stir in the chilli, the tomatoes and the spices and cook for 1 min. Remove from the heat and divide into four.
2 Heat a little oil in the frying pan, add one quarter of the tomato mixture to the pan, then pour in a quarter of the beaten eggs.
3 Cook over a medium heat pushing the cooked egg towards the centre of the pan until no runny egg remains. Cook for a min more until the base is golden.
4 Fold the omelette in the pan and tip onto a warm plate. Garnish with chopped coriander.
5 Repeat to make 3 more omelettes in the same way.
British Lion Eggs eggrecipes.co.uk

20 SUNDAY

21 MONDAY

22 TUESDAY

23 WEDNESDAY

24 THURSDAY

25 FRIDAY

26 SATURDAY

Down memory lane

SUNDAY SCHOOL TWICE OVER

I used to go to two Sunday Schools. One was held on a Sunday morning in a lovely old church on top of a hill and the other one was in the afternoon at the local chapel.

I was reluctant to give up the morning Sunday School because I was in the choir and earned two shillings for singing at weddings, but the Girls' Life Brigade which I had joined after our Girl Guides troupe disbanded was attached to the chapel.

One sunny day when some of us didn't feel like sitting indoors in the church hall, we hid behind a gravestone then crept out once the coast was clear. We were found out when my sister tripped over a hidden pipe, fell, and fractured her arm on a marble headstone. She was in plaster for ages and as the older sibling I got the blame for leading her astray.

A good thing about going to two Sunday Schools was that we had two annual outings and two Christmas parties!
Gill Maughan, Plymouth

Name that tune

Moving hearts and minds in the midst of the Second World War, this optimistic song made a sweetheart of its singer and was also given to a 1943 musical of the same name.

A: We'll Meet Again, Vera Lynn

Word of the week

Floccinaucinihilipilification

This mouthful of a word refers to the act of 'considering something to be not at all important', or 'estimating something as useless'. Being so tricky to spell, as a word it isn't all that useful!

Try something new!

Make a travel scrapbook. Stick down photos, write down words, quotes or dates and add stickers, postcards, tickets and travel souvenirs to the pages of a blank wire bound book. Use colourful card and pens to help evoke memories of the aromas, ambience and temperature.

Uncommon knowledge

One of the neighbours James Stewart spies upon in Hitchcock's Rear Window, is none other than the composer Ross Bagdasarian. Bagdasarian is perhaps most well known as the creator of the musical rodents, Alvin and the Chipmunks.

Recipe of the week

ROAST CHICKEN & TOMATO CHICKPEA TRAY BAKE

SERVES: 2
PREP: 5 mins
COOK: 45 mins

4 bone-in chicken thighs
300g (10½oz) cherry tomatoes
1 x 355g jar of Odysea chickpeas in tomato sauce
50ml (1¾ fl oz) water
Extra-virgin olive oil
Salt and pepper
100g (4oz) spinach

1 Pre-heat the oven to 200°C/Fan 180°C/Gas Mark 6.
2 Put the chicken, cherry tomatoes and the jar of chickpeas with the water into an ovenproof dish, drizzle with a little extra-virgin olive oil and season with salt and pepper.
3 Bake for 45 mins and serve over the spinach.
Easy Peasy Baking fabflour.co.uk

27 SUNDAY

28 MONDAY

1 TUESDAY

2 WEDNESDAY

3 THURSDAY

4 FRIDAY

5 SATURDAY

Down memory lane

TOOTH PULLER IN CHIEF

Our school janitor, Mr Whittet, was a kindly man; tall and thin, ramrod straight with short grey hair and blue eyes. He wore a smart dark navy uniform with brass buttons and a peaked cap.

He knew every child by their first name. Apart from his normal duties, he wiped away many a tear and cleaned many grazed knees. He was also a peacekeeper who made sure that any playground squabbles were quickly squashed. But his most spectacular role was as a dentist.

If you had a wobbly tooth, the thing to do was to see Mr Whittet. Reaching into his pocket, he would pull out a pristine white hankie then ask you to open wide. Placing it over the offending tooth, he moved it back and forth. If the tooth wasn't ready to come out, he told you to come back the following day. It was always a disappointment when your tooth fell out overnight because, strange as it may seem, we wanted Mr Whittet to perform the task. To this day, he is remembered with great fondness by all who knew him.
Margaret Mather, via email

Name that tune

This dreamy tune, a hit with parents, told of the warmth of Los Angeles, bitterly missed in the cold of New York City.

A: California Dreamin', the Mamas and the Papas

Word of the week

Twig

Word origins are not always easy to establish, particularly with words that have multiple meanings. As a noun a twig is a small branch and can be traced back to Old Norse. As a verb, to twig is to suddenly understand something and is thought to have Gaelic roots.

Try something new!

Volunteer with your local nature conservation charity. From building hedgehog houses to restoring sand dunes, take some time out to help support British wildlife and its wonderful habitats. Get involved in a project near you at wildlifetrusts.org/volunteering-opportunities

Uncommon knowledge

In How to Marry a Millionaire, when Lauren Bacall is attempting to convince William Powell that she likes older men, she refers to the "old fellow" in African Queen whom she's crazy about. Which is of course Humphrey Bogart, her real-life husband.

Recipe of the week

HEALTHY FISH & NEW POTATO CHIPS

SERVES: 2
PREP: 15 mins
COOK: 30-35 mins

650g (1lb 7oz) new/baby potatoes
70g (2½oz) breadcrumbs
Zest of ½ lemon and a wedge to serve
1 tbsp chopped parsley
Salt and pepper
20g (¾oz) butter
2 tbsp vegetable oil
2 fillets of white fish (cod or haddock)
200g (7oz) frozen peas
1 tbsp mint sauce
Tartare sauce to serve (optional)
1 tbsp capers (optional)

1 Pre-heat the oven to 190°C/Fan 170°C/Gas Mark 5. Peel and chop the potatoes into small sticks. Bring a large saucepan of salted water to the boil and par boil the potatoes for 5 mins.
2 Place the breadcrumbs in a bowl and add the lemon zest, chopped parsley, salt and pepper. Melt 14g (½oz) of butter and stir through the breadcrumb mixture to combine.
3 Take a large oven tray, pour in the vegetable oil and place in the oven. Place the fish fillets on a small oven tray. Season and pop a knob of butter on each and cover with foil.
4 Remove the large oven tray and add the potatoes. Mix around to coat in the oil, then season. Place both trays in the oven.
5 After 15 mins remove the foil from the fish and cover each fish with the breadcrumbs. Give the chips a shake. Place both back in oven for a further 10-15 mins.
6 Meanwhile make the crushed peas. Add the peas to boiling water. Once cooked, slightly mash and add the mint sauce. Serve with a slice of lemon and the tartare sauce topped with extra capers.

seasonalspuds.com

6 SUNDAY

_____

7 MONDAY

_____

8 TUESDAY

_____

9 WEDNESDAY

_____

10 THURSDAY

_____

11 FRIDAY

_____

12 SATURDAY

_____

Down memory lane

OUR COSY CARAVAN

When I was married in 1958 we lived in a bedsit in Leytonstone but my husband, who was in the RAF, was stationed in Chigwell and I worked at Stratford.

One morning on my way to work I noticed a pink caravan for sale in a garage car park. Knowing my husband would soon be posted to a new station near Sheffield, I told him about it. We decided to buy the caravan. Everything for our move was arranged by the Air Force.

The site we were on was small with no running water or electricity. We had a coal fire so it was warm and cosy inside the caravan. When we ran out of coal we walked to the local coal mine and bought what we needed. We made several friends who also lived on the site and often played cards and games with them.

In the bitterly cold weather, the tap near the toilet block froze. On several occasions the bus that my husband caught to work couldn't get through because of the snow and the bus driver was glad when he and other passengers helped to dig him out!

Doreen Croxon, Histon

Name that tune

Inspired by gospel music, this song spent six weeks at No 1, despite causing non-stop 'trouble' for the duo that recorded it. It was later covered by everyone from Elvis Presley to Aretha Franklin.

A: Bridge Over Troubled Water, Simon and Garfunkel

Word of the week

Gardyloo
This Scottish word was a shout you'd once hear regularly across the streets of Edinburgh. The cry would warn passers-by to move out of the way, as dirty water from chamber pots was emptied out of windows onto the streets below.

Try something new!
Forage for wild food. Get out into the countryside and keep your eyes peeled for bushes full of blackberries, fruit trees with apples, plums or pears or even sweet-smelling wild garlic underfoot. Do your research on what's safe to eat before you go and get the land owner's permission.

Uncommon knowledge

Known by many as the 'Fifth Beatle', Brian Epstein managed some of music's biggest acts: Billy J Kramer and the Dakotas; Gerry and the Pacemakers; and of course, The Beatles. The Beatles and Epstein's original contract sold at auction for £240,000.

Recipe of the week

TRIO OF FISH PIE

SERVES: 4
PREP: 15 mins
COOK: 20 mins

500g (1lb 2oz) Charlotte potatoes, thinly sliced
25g (1oz) unsalted butter
25g (1oz) plain flour
300ml (½ pt) semi-skimmed milk
75g (3oz) light soft cheese
1 tsp salt
1 tsp wholegrain mustard
25g (1oz) chives, chopped
500g (1lb 2oz) diced mixed cod, salmon, cooked prawns

1 Pre-heat the oven to 200°C/Fan 180°C/Gas Mark 6.
2 Cook the potatoes in boiling water for 5 mins, drain.
3 Meanwhile, melt the butter in a medium saucepan and add the flour, cook for 30 secs. Gradually whisk in the milk and bring to the boil, stirring until thickened. Add soft cheese, salt, mustard and chives.
4 Stir the fish into the sauce and cook for 2-3 mins, transfer to an ovenproof serving dish. Top with the potatoes and season with black pepper. Bake for 20 mins until golden.
Losalt.com

13 SUNDAY

14 MONDAY

15 TUESDAY

16 WEDNESDAY

17 THURSDAY

18 FRIDAY

19 SATURDAY

Down memory lane

HIGH TEA ON SUNDAY

The youngest in a family of five sisters and three brothers, I have happy memories of our Sundays in the Thirties. On the days when I was not attending Sunday School, I would cycle to visit my cousins who lived locally. If the weather was bad, I used to curl up in a chair with a book instead.

In the afternoon, Mother would come downstairs wearing a dress and a pretty frilly apron in readiness for the arrival of visitors for high tea. Together we set the table which we covered with an elegant damask tablecloth. Usually we had a full house of family and friends, my brothers brought their girlfriends and my sisters brought their boyfriends, all in their Sunday best. The men wore starched white collars (very uncomfortable) with cufflinks and armbands.

It was good that we spent those times together for little did we realise that life was to change dramatically. Soon the country was at war and many of my family were in uniform, serving in the army or as air-raid wardens, while my parents and grandparents took in evacuees from the cities.

Velma Munns, Wellingborough

Name that tune

As Fred and Ginger twirl around the floor in one of the cleverest dance routines in history this song croons along, so good it makes our heart beat so fast we're lost for words.

A: Cheek to Cheek, by Irving Berlin

Word of the week

Scurryfunge

If you've been busy spring cleaning your home, you won't need to complete a 'scurryfunge' when someone next pays you a visit. This unusual word describes the frantic dash to tidy up before guests arrive.

Try something new!

Find some funky fungi. Take to the woods or your back garden for a fungi hunt. Wild mushrooms come in all different shapes and sizes - and some have silly names too. Take your sketchbook or camera along on your fungi hunt to keep a diary of your discoveries and research their species on your return.

Uncommon knowledge

The infamous Oddjob, from Bond film Goldfinger, was played by weightlifter Harold Sakata. This would not be Sakata's only appearance in an Ian Fleming film, as he would later appear in Danger Grows Wild (1966), directed by Terence Young.

Recipe of the week

CLASSIC SCONES

SERVES: 8
PREP: 10 mins
COOK: 10-12 mins

200g (7oz) self-raising flour
30g (1oz) caster sugar
60g (2oz) unsalted butter, chilled and cubed
2 eggs (1 is for eggwash)
2 tbsp milk

1 Pre-heat the oven to 180°C/Fan 160°C/Gas Mark 4 and line the baking tray with the parchment.
2 Combine the flour and sugar in a bowl, then add in the butter cubes and work them in with your fingers to make a crumb consistency.
3 Make a well in the centre and add 1 egg and the milk. Bring it all together until just combined to form a dough, being careful not to overwork it.
4 Tip the dough out onto a lightly floured surface and roll out to a 1in (2cm) thickness, cut out rounds, bringing the offcuts together and re-rolling until you have 8 rounds.
5 Place them all on the baking tray, rub the tops with eggwash and bake in the oven for 10-12 mins until risen and golden on top.
6 Cool and serve with jam and clotted cream.

Easy Peasy Baking fabflour.co.uk

20 SUNDAY

21 MONDAY

22 TUESDAY

23 WEDNESDAY

24 THURSDAY

25 FRIDAY

26 SATURDAY

Down memory lane

WE MISSED MARMITE

This photo was taken in 1975 on the island of Bougainville in Papua New Guinea. It was at the Independence Day celebration known locally as Sing Sing. My daughter was three years old and doesn't look very impressed.

My husband's work at a large copper mine on the island had taken us there. Before that I had never been abroad or on an aeroplane. Needless to say, it was initially a huge culture shock. We lived in a company house in a township built in the middle of a tropical jungle. Our neighbours were a mixture of different nationalities.

The lifestyle was quite colonial. We had a country club, a sports centre and an amateur dramatic society as well as fabulous beaches, local markets and other islands to visit. We Brits were always excited to hear that a cargo ship had arrived from the UK as that meant we could buy Branston pickle, Marmite and Heinz baked beans at the one supermarket in the town.
Patricia Daniels, via email

Name that tune

A country song about a condemned prisoner, this was made into more of a pop hit by a smooth tiger who said the lyrics made him think of his beloved Welsh hometown.

A: Green Green Grass of Home, by Tom Jones

Word of the week

Happiness

The word happiness comes from the Old Norse term hap, which means luck or chance and is linked to an Old English term meaning equal. Chance and equality both seem a good place to start in the search for true happiness.

Try something new!

Try a new cuisine you've never tasted before. Use Google to source a recipe, dig out an old cookbook or sign up to a meal kit subscription company such as HelloFresh or Gousto. They deliver fresh ingredients and recipe cards for a variety of international cuisines direct to your door.

Uncommon knowledge

Paul Simon and Art Garfunkel's iconic The Sound of Silence was not originally a hit. Its first acoustic version was on the album Wednesday Morning, 3AM which flopped. It was only when, unbeknown to the duo, the label remixed it with electronic instruments and released it as a single did it hit the charts at No 1. The pair had split up by this point, but the success convinced them to reunite, and they would go on to record four more albums together.

Recipe of the week

CHICKEN MASSAMAN CURRY

SERVES: 4
PREP: 15 mins
COOK: 20-25 mins

400ml (14oz) can reduced-fat coconut milk
200ml (7 fl oz) chicken stock
100g (4oz) jar Cooks' Ingredients Massaman Thai Curry Paste
1 cinnamon stick
6 chicken thigh fillets
300g (10oz) Waitrose Miniature Potatoes, halved
50g (2oz) cashew nuts or peanuts
1 red chilli
½ x 28g (1oz) pack fresh coriander, leaves only
2 salad onions, shredded
Cooked basmati rice, to serve
1 lime, cut into wedges

1 Place the coconut milk, stock, curry paste and cinnamon stick in a large saucepan and bring to a simmer. Cut the chicken into cubes and add to the pan with the potatoes. Cook gently for 20-25 mins until the potatoes are tender and the chicken is cooked through.
2 Meanwhile, toast the cashew nuts or peanuts in a small non-stick frying pan for 3-4 mins. Deseed the chilli and slice it into long shreds. Set aside.
3 Divide the curry among 4 bowls and scatter with the toasted nuts, coriander leaves, chilli and salad onions. Serve with rice and lime wedges for squeezing over.
Waitrose.com

27 SUNDAY

28 MONDAY

29 TUESDAY

30 WEDNESDAY

31 THURSDAY

1 FRIDAY

2 SATURDAY

Down memory lane

A CHEEKY PROMISE

Although some people didn't like prefabs and called them rabbit hutches, at the end of the war my parents were glad to be given the keys to view one. The roads and pavements weren't finished and there were no garden fences, but my mother was pleased to find that the kitchen was big enough to have a table and chairs.

In 1956 I left home to get married and five years after that my husband and I were given a prefab two rows away from the one I had grown up in. As the walls were only made of a compressed material, my little boy and his friend found it easy and fun to make a big hole in one of the outside walls. Hearing them at it again, I shouted: "Stop it at once or I really will smack your bottom!" I turned bright red when the workmen who had come to mend the damage called back: "Promises, promises!"

This picture of me (in the middle) was taken outside our prefab. They have all gone now, but the prefabs lasted a lot longer than their intended lifespan of ten years.
Coral Murphy, Canterbury

Name that tune

Originally the soaring conclusion to a much-loved Rogers and Hammerstein musical, this song is now better known by sporting fans or for its more recent association with an unlikely hero who became famous aged 100.

A: You'll Never Walk Alone,
Gerry & the Pacemakers

Word of the week

Facetiously

Pronounced fah-see-shuhs-lee, it's the act of deliberately jesting or joking about something inappropriately. What makes it so special is that it contains all the vowels in the correct alphabetical order, plus the semivowel 'y'.

Try something new!

Keep a nature diary. Writing things down is a brilliant way to notice patterns and changes in your garden or surrounding area. Note the time, date and place and what you see. Should you want to, use a website such as iSpot (ispotnature.org) to upload photos for experts to identify.

Uncommon knowledge

In early drafts of Return of the Jedi, the final battle was meant to take place on and above Chewbacca's home world of Kashyyyk. Quickly realising the cost of making so many 6ft fur costumes, they instead settled for the humble Ewok, this one played by a young Warwick Davis.

Recipe of the week

CHERRY, CHOCOLATE, GINGER & MARSHMALLOW TRAY BAKE

SERVES: 10
PREP TIME: 15 mins

200g (7oz) dark chocolate
100g (4oz) butter
1 tbsp Opies Stem Ginger syrup (from the jar)
200g (7oz) digestive biscuits
1 jar Opies Cocktail Cherries, drained and halved
100g (4oz) mini marshmallows
2 pieces of Opies Stem Ginger, finely sliced
2 pieces of Opies Crystallised Ginger, finely sliced

1 Line a standard loaf tin with cling film, making sure to leave an overhang so you can easily remove the cake.
2 In a bowl break the chocolate, add the butter and golden syrup and microwave on low power. Stir every 20 secs until the chocolate and butter have melted. Leave to one side.
3 In a mixing bowl, break the digestive biscuits into large chunks. Then add the cherries, marshmallows, stem ginger and crystallised ginger.
4 Pour over the chocolate and mix well.
5 Spoon the mixture into the prepared loaf tin and press down gently. Pop into the fridge for a couple of hours to set.
6 Once set, lift out the cake from the tin using the overhang of cling film. Slice and serve.

opiesfoods.com

3 SUNDAY

4 MONDAY

5 TUESDAY

6 WEDNESDAY

7 THURSDAY

8 FRIDAY

9 SATURDAY

Down memory lane

A VERY SPECIAL BABY

This photo is of me with my adoptive parents. I was one of many babies born as the result of a romantic liaison during the war. My birth mother worked on an American army camp as a telephonist while her husband was away fighting for king and country. When he was told about the baby, he said that she must have it adopted.

So along came Mum and Dad. In those days you were allowed to meet the birth mother around the date when the baby was due. The midwife opened the door and said: "You are just in time, the baby has been born" so they were able to hold me when I was just half-an-hour old.

Three months later I was legally adopted and we moved to London where I grew up. When I was five years old they sat me down and told me I was very special because they couldn't have any children of their own. Aged 12, I told this story with pride at my school assembly. Many years later, I happened to bump into one of my former teachers who told me he'd never forgotten my speech which he found very moving.

Sheila Lead, New Milton

Name that tune

Written by Doc Pomus when he couldn't dance with his bride on his wedding day because polio had left him on crutches, this was a big hit for an American doo-wop group.

A: Save the Last Dance For Me, The Drifters

Word of the week

Withershins

Sometimes called widdershins, it means travelling or moving in a direction contrary to the usual or a direction contrary to the apparent course of the sun. In other words, moving anti-clockwise.

Try something new!

Go for an outdoor swim. The UK is filled with lots of lovely open-air lidos for taking a cool, refreshing dip. If you're feeling daring, wildswimming.co.uk has lots of information on swimming spots for beginners, including rivers, lakes, waterfalls and streams and how to visit them safely.

Uncommon knowledge

In Reach for the Sky, to portray RAF ace Douglas Bader, Kenneth More had his legs encased in aluminium to more accurately reflect Bader's own injuries. More's next film would see him in A Night to Remember (1958), a Titanic biopic.

Recipe of the week

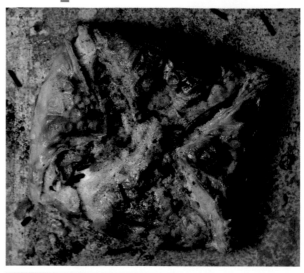

EASY TUNA & EGG LUNCHBOX PASTIES

SERVES: 4
PREP: 25 mins
COOK: 40 mins

4 medium eggs
500g (1lb 1oz) pack puff pastry
350g (12oz) tub Waitrose Four Cheese Sauce
2 x 160g (5½ oz) cans John West Pole & Line Caught Tuna Chunks In Spring Water, drained
25g (1oz) pack chives, snipped
Plain flour, for rolling
½ tsp cayenne or paprika, to serve

1 Cook 3 of the eggs in a saucepan of boiling water for 9 mins. Drain and cool a little under running water then peel and roughly chop.
2 Meanwhile, pre-heat the oven to 200°C/Fan 180°C/Gas Mark 6.
3 Flour a surface. Roll out the pastry to make a 38cm (14in) square and cut into 4 squares. Beat the remaining egg.
4 Mix the chopped eggs, cheese sauce, tuna and most of the chives. Divide the filling between the pastry squares, brush the edges with beaten egg then pull the four corners up and inward to meet in the centre, folding one corner over the other like closing an envelope. Firmly press the edges together to seal (using more beaten egg if you need). Repeat to make 4 parcels.
5 Transfer the parcels to a parchment-lined baking sheet and brush lightly with egg. Bake for 25-30 mins until golden. Scatter a pinch of cayenne or paprika and chives onto each pasty and serve.
waitrose.com

10 SUNDAY

11 MONDAY

12 TUESDAY

13 WEDNESDAY

14 THURSDAY

15 FRIDAY

16 SATURDAY

Down memory lane

KNIT ONE, PURL ONE

This is my mum, Marjorie, who sadly passed away at the age of 96. In 1956, when I was ten, she went out to work full-time in a wool shop in Brighouse, West Yorkshire. The building was a wooden hut divided into two, the other half being a sweet shop. Mum's shop not only sold wool and accessories such as knitting needles and patterns, but also sanitary towels and nylons. The nylons were displayed on a wooden leg in the window.

In those days, a customer could choose her wool and have it put away so she could go in and buy a few ounces at a time. The wool came in hanks that had to be wound into balls with one person holding the hank between their hands while the other did the winding. When there weren't any customers, Mum had to knit men's socks on a machine in the back room. No lounging about for her!

After she died we found the knitting machine in a cupboard where it had been for 50 years. The wooden hut had long ago been demolished to make way for the entrance to a car park.
Patricia Mason, via email

Name that tune

When a little girl with flaming locks of auburn hair and eyes of emerald green turned up at an autograph signing, little did she realise she would inspire this classic song by a country legend.

A: Jolene, Dolly Parton

Word of the week

Dauncy

Pronounced 'dawn-see', you might also see dauncy spelt as donsie, donsey and a few other ways too. Although not widely used now, dauncy was once commonly used in Scotland and northern England as a way of describing someone who was weak, feeble or feeling unwell.

Try something new!

Walk barefoot. It's the perfect activity for exploring the great outdoors and making a lasting connection with nature. Clamber up beach dunes and feel the warm sand on your soles, dance on soft dewy grass in your garden or listen to the squelching of wet mud squishing underfoot.

Uncommon knowledge

In Brother Rat (1938) about military cadets, two of its stars would serve in the Second World War, including Eddie Albert who would rise to the rank of Lieutenant. Not forgetting of course, Ronald Reagan, future honorary Brother Rat and President to be.

Recipe of the week

LAMB & NEW POTATO TRAYBAKE

SERVES: 4
PREP: 10 mins
COOK: 55 mins

1kg (35oz) new/baby potatoes
8 lamb cutlets
1 whole fennel bulb
1 whole lemon cut into wedges
20ml olive oil
2 tbsp mint sauce
Juice of ½ a lemon
Salt and pepper
200g (7oz) frozen peas
Couple of sprigs of fresh mint

1 Pre-heat the oven to 180°C/Fan 160°C/Gas Mark 4.
2 Bring a large pan of salted water to the boil, and par boil the potatoes (whole) for 10 mins.
3 Place the potatoes and lamb cutlets in a large oven tray. Cut the fennel into wedges and add these along with the lemon wedges.
4 Mix the olive oil with the mint sauce and pour it over the traybake with the lemon juice.
5 Cook in the pre-heated oven for 30 mins.
6 Remove from the oven, turn the lamb over, and mix all the other ingredients. Season. Add the frozen peas and place back in the oven for a further 15 mins.
7 Serve with a couple of sprigs of fresh mint.
seasonalspuds.com

17 SUNDAY

18 MONDAY

19 TUESDAY

20 WEDNESDAY

21 THURSDAY

22 FRIDAY

23 SATURDAY

Down memory lane

EASTER IN EXETER

The church in this photo is St Mary's in the city of Exeter where I attended a convent school. Once a week during Lent our class would walk down Fore Street to the church where we assembled in the pews to await Father Brown. After prayers and a hymn we formed a procession and performed the Stations of the Cross, kneeling and praying at each plaque which portrayed the stages of Jesus's progress to the cross. On Easter Sunday the cathedral bells of St Peter would ring full peal and could be heard across the city.

My mother made Easter eggs for my sister and me although mine had to be made without chocolate as I have always been allergic to cocoa. There were cycle rides into the countryside with a friend to pick wild daffodils to take home for our mothers.

Later, when I was married, although Good Friday was a solemn day when our family always attended church, on Sunday my son and daughter had fun laughing at the Easter bonnets each of them had made at school.
Sheila Mills, Minehead

Name that tune

Originally a heart-warming hit for Dionne Warwick, this became the song that shot a chirpy Liverpudlian lass with a later talent for TV dating shows to the No 1 spot.

A: Anyone Who Had a Heart, Cilla Black

Word of the week

Wabbit

You'd be forgiven for assuming wabbit referred to the cute and fluffy kind, after all everyone's favourite 'wascally wabbit' was Bugs Bunny. In fact, wabbit means feeling very tired, weak and unhealthy.

Try something new!

Try a new type of puzzle. For example, if you love sudoku, give kakuro a go.

Uncommon knowledge

Disney's iron grip over its properties has become legendary, but it held on to none so tight as Snow White. Adriana Caselotti, the actress behind Snow White, had such a unique voice that Disney, in effect, copyrighted it, stopping her from performing in any other roles and largely ending her career after Snow White and the Seven Dwarfs.

Recipe of the week

HOT CROSS BUNS

MAKES: 12
PREP: 15 mins (plus 1½ hours proving time)
COOK: 25 mins

450g (16oz) strong white bread flour
1 tsp salt
2 tsp mixed spice
100g (4oz) caster sugar
7g sachet easy blend dried yeast
250g (9oz) dried mixed fruit
50g (2oz) butter
250ml (0.25l) milk plus 3 tbsp
1 large Lion Quality egg, beaten
50g (2oz) plain flour
1 tbsp veg oil for oiling the clingfilm

1 Sift the flour, salt, spice and 50g of the sugar in a large bowl. Stir in the yeast and fruit. In a small pan, melt the butter, then add the milk and heat until tepid. Stir into the dry ingredients with the egg and mix to form a soft dough.
2 Tip the dough out on a floured work surface and knead for 10 mins. Divide into 12 equal pieces and shape each into a ball. Place on an oiled baking sheet, cover with oiled clingfilm and leave to prove in a warm place for about 1½ hours until doubled in size.
3 Pre-heat the oven to 190°C/Fan 170°C/Gas Mark 5. To make the crosses, put the plain flour in a small bowl with 6 tbsp cold water; mix to a smooth paste. Spoon into a piping bag and neatly pipe a cross over each of the buns. Bake for 20-25 mins or until golden brown.
4 Heat the remaining sugar and milk with 3 tbsp water in a small pan, stirring until the sugar dissolves. Boil for 1 min. Remove the buns from the oven and brush twice with the glaze. Leave to cool on a wire rack. Serve warm spread with butter.

British Lion Eggs eggrecipes.co.uk

24 SUNDAY

25 MONDAY

26 TUESDAY

27 WEDNESDAY

28 THURSDAY

29 FRIDAY

30 SATURDAY

Down memory lane

THE MAGIC OF STEAM

This is me, aged six, with my mum. My dad was the station master at Killay in South Wales and I still remember the day he took me to work with him. Before we boarded the train in Swansea, Dad went to talk with the engine driver who invited me up on to the footplate. I was thrilled, but when the fireman opened the door to put on more coal, the heat terrified me!

We were the only two people in our compartment and the velour seats tickled the backs of my knees. The train travelled along the coast with beautiful views of Mumbles before crossing the bridge at Blackpill into Clyne Valley woods. In the woods was a cottage and Dad threw a shopping bag through the window to land in the garden. The owner waved to us. Later, he would bring the bag to Killay station filled with fresh free-range eggs.

While Dad worked, I was allowed out on the platform, standing well back, to watch the trains approaching. There was noise, steam and the slamming of carriage doors, then the driver waited until the guard raised his green flag and blew his whistle before proceeding.

Pam Brannigan, Swansea

Name that tune

When a legendary performer found himself in times of difficulty, he dreamt of his mother Mary and made a song about her that became the final single before the world's biggest band drifted apart.

A: Let It Be, The Beatles

Word of the week

Groggy

Old Grog was the nickname of Admiral Edward Vernon, an 18th Century British Royal Navy commander. The Admiral's nickname came from a cloak he wore made from coarse grogram. He also rationed his crew's alcohol by watering down their rum and this 'grog' prevented them feeling 'groggy' the morning after!

Try something new!

Complete a random act of kindness – research shows it can be beneficial to our mental health. Bake a cake for a neighbour, give a friend a compliment, pay for a stranger's drink at a café, or let someone go before you in a queue! No matter how big or small, it's the thought that counts.

Uncommon knowledge

Stormy Weather (1943) features Lena Horne, Bill Robinson, and Cab Calloway alongside many terrific songs and dance routines. Fred Astaire was so impressed by the Nicholas Brothers' Jumpin' Jive routine that he called it "the greatest movie musical number I have ever seen."

Recipe of the week

RHUBARB & STRAWBERRY CRUMBLE

SERVES: 6
PREP: 15 mins
COOK: 45 mins

400g (14oz) rhubarb, cut into 3cm lengths
400g (14oz) strawberries, hulled and halved
2 star anise
75g light brown soft sugar
Grated zest and juice of 1 large orange
For the topping:
150g (5oz) porridge oats
100g (4oz) plain flour
100g (4oz) chilled butter, diced
2 tbsp clear honey
100g (4oz) light brown soft sugar
50g (2oz) roasted chopped hazelnuts

1 Pre-heat the oven to 180°C/ Fan 160°C /Gas Mark 4. Place the rhubarb, strawberries, star anise, sugar, orange zest and juice in a large ovenproof dish.
2 Place the oats, flour and butter in a bowl then, using your fingertips, rub in the butter until it resembles breadcrumbs. Add the honey, sugar and hazelnuts then rub together to form small clumps.
3 Scatter the oaty crumble over the fruit. Sit the dish on a baking sheet in the oven and cook for 45 mins until the fruit is tender, bubbling around the edges and the top is crunchy and golden brown.
Waitrose.com

1 SUNDAY

2 MONDAY

3 TUESDAY

4 WEDNESDAY

5 THURSDAY

6 FRIDAY

7 SATURDAY

Down memory lane

TOYS WERE US

This photo is of me with my son Martin, aged two. I can't believe the size of my glasses - they remind me of Deirdre Barlow in Coronation Street! The picture was taken in the early Nineties when I had opened a shop selling new and used baby goods. At that time there were fewer charity shops and as my husband had been facing the possibility of redundancy I hoped it would give us some extra income.

It was very much a family collaboration. My husband, who was good at DIY, used to mend any second-hand nursery equipment requiring repairs. I was meticulous in making sure that all used items were clean and safe. I printed my own flyers which my elder son posted through doors. We used to check to make sure all the pieces were in the jigsaws and board games and also read all the children's books. Martin loved testing out the toys - he had everything from farm animals to a fort. He enjoyed the Fisher Price toys that were popular then. Recently I sent our eight-year-old grandson some Star Wars figures that I've kept all these years.
Janet Dandy, Burnley

Name that tune

You must remember this one. A dreamily romantic song originally intended for a Broadway musical but now best associated with a Humphrey Bogart and Ingrid Bergman movie about a big Moroccan city.

A: As Time Goes By, Dooley Wilson

Word of the week

Gasconade

This word has a lot to say about itself. Gasconade means extravagant boasting, or refers to boastful talk. Gasconade County is also a small county in the US state of Missouri.

Try something new!

Learn a new word from the dictionary. Do this every day for one week. Don't have a copy? Visit dictionary.com and view the 'word of the day' on the homepage with a brief description of its meaning.

Uncommon knowledge

Despite being a low-budget film, The Raven (1963), sported quite an all-star cast: Vincent Price, Peter Lorre, Boris Karloff, and a young Jack Nicholson.

This comedy horror about rival wizards was well received, Jack Nicholson had high praise for those he worked with, apart from one. The titular bird had found a use of its own for Nicholson, who said: "I would look down when the Raven flew off my shoulder, and it would be covered in poop. I hated that bird."

Recipe of the week

ATLANTIC SALMON & ASPARAGUS SALAD

SERVES: 4
PREP: 6 mins
COOK: 4 mins

4 handfuls of watercress
4 asparagus spears, shaved lengthways
8 tsp ricotta
1 lemon, zest and juice
Salt and pepper
1 handful of frozen peas
4 large eggs
Olive oil
2 x 160g cans Princes Skinless & Boneless Atlantic Salmon in Brine

1 Get a large serving plate and start by adding a layer of watercress.
2 Shave lengths of asparagus using a potato peeler and add those to the salad.
3 Mix the ricotta with a squeeze of lemon, a grating of lemon zest and a pinch of salt and pepper, then dollop the ricotta randomly around the salad.
4 Defrost some peas and then add to the salad.
5 Bring a pan of water to the boil and gently poach 4 eggs for 4 mins each, by adding them to the water using a teacup and gently lowering them in.
6 Break up chunks of the Princes Atlantic Salmon and add to the salad. Add the poached eggs and serve with a drizzle of olive oil, and a pinch of salt and pepper.

Miguel Barclay/Princes princes.co.uk

8 SUNDAY

9 MONDAY

10 TUESDAY

11 WEDNESDAY

12 THURSDAY

13 FRIDAY

14 SATURDAY

Down memory lane

MY DEAR DAD, ALBERT

My dad joined the London Fire Brigade in 1938 but this picture was taken before that when he was a bandsman with the First Battalion of the Lancashire Loyals, stationed in India. He played the drums as well as brass instruments and in later years enlivened our big family parties playing the piano.

As a fireman based in the City of London during the war Dad was often in danger. Because there was always the possibility he wouldn't return home, he taught me basic DIY jobs. Mum was a great homemaker but she couldn't change a light bulb or mend a fuse! At Christmas, he used to 'run up' paper chains on Mum's Singer sewing machine, ice the cake and seal the pudding ready for steaming.

Dad was a very patient man and spent hours with my daughters doing drawings, telling stories and playing tunes with his drumsticks on the arm of his chair. Even after he was retired he could still ride a bicycle backwards or with no hands so the local boys would knock on the door and ask Mum: "Can Albert come out to play?"!
Jill Montgomery, Dover

Name that tune

Some say this was written about Caroline Kennedy while others say the singer wanted to dedicate a song to his wife Marcia but her name didn't fit the sweet melody, so he picked a different name.

A: Sweet Caroline, Neil Diamond

Word of the week

Triskaidekaphobia

Is the fear of the number 13. Superstition surrounding this number is thought to be rooted in Christianity, after Judas was the 13th guest at the Last Supper. Another equally hard to pronounce word paraskevidekatriaphobia, is superstition of Friday the 13th. Luckily only one falls in the year of 2022 (May 13th).

Try something new!

Organise a clothing swap with your friends. You'll have a great time, save some pennies and help out the environment all at the same time.

Uncommon knowledge

Though afterwards they became good friends, Julie Andrews and Christopher Plummer's rivalry on the set of The Sound of Music was legendary. Plummer was particularly vocal on this matter, and often referred to the film as The Sound of Mucus, and Andrews as Ms Disney.

Recipe of the week

SPINACH, FETA & PINE NUT OMELETTE

SERVES: 1
PREP: 5 mins
COOK: 5 mins

1 tbsp olive or coconut oil
100g (4oz) bag of baby spinach, washed
2 British Lion eggs
30g (1oz) feta cheese, diced fairly small
1 tbsp toasted pine nuts

1 Heat the oil in a small non-stick frying pan. Add the spinach and allow it to wilt in the heat of the pan – about 3 mins.
2 Add the beaten eggs and mix everything around in the pan.
3 As soon as the eggs start to set tip in the feta cheese and the pine nuts. Continue turning everything around in the pan for a min or so.
4 Leave the pan on the heat until the outside is starting to go a golden brown colour.
5 Place a plate over the pan and hold it down securely. Lift the pan and turn it over so that the omelette is on the plate.
6 Slide the omelette back into the pan and cook the other side, then serve when ready.

British Lion Eggs eggrecipes.co.uk

15 SUNDAY

16 MONDAY

17 TUESDAY

18 WEDNESDAY

19 THURSDAY

20 FRIDAY

21 SATURDAY

Down memory lane

HEAVEN CAN WAIT!

This picture is of me and my twin brother dressed ready for Sunday School. Our Auntie Francis used to take us. I sat on the back of her bicycle, legs dangling each side of the back wheel, while my brother pedalled like mad on his bike to keep alongside.

Chobham Gospel Hall was a corrugated iron building that always smelled musty. The preacher, a rather cross-looking man, and his wife were in charge. She played the organ and he told us about Jesus and how our souls would go to Heaven, but only if we were good. I imagined our souls were like the soles on the bottom of our shoes so I decided to be naughty sometimes then Heaven wouldn't want me.

At the end of the lesson we were told that the world will end one day and we would all be saved. When the preacher asked if anyone knew when that would happen, my hand shot up and I said: "No-one knows." To my amazement, I was told that this was the right answer and I was awarded the prize of a pencil and a rubber.
Pamela Wareing, Hayling Island

Name that tune

Be quiet – but only absent-mindedly. This song features one of the best-known saxophone solos there is, written when the performer, then just 17, was on the bus on his way to the 'silver screen'.

A: Careless Whisper, Wham!

Word of the week

Nice

Not the most exciting word in the English language, 'nice' wasn't always a compliment. During the 14th Century it meant ignorant or foolish, then over time it became a term for someone who dressed extravagantly, before becoming the rather neutral compliment it is today!

Try something new!

Meditate. Find a quiet corner - inside or out - take a seat, get comfortable and set a time limit. Notice the sensation in your body, feel your breath and acknowledge thoughts as they come and go. For extra guidance, download the Headspace app (headspace.com) for a free trial of short sessions.

Uncommon knowledge

For the lighthouse scenes in Pete's Dragon, Disney had built a 52ft lighthouse on a hiking trail in California. The beacon used was so powerful that they had to acquire special permission from the Coast Guard as it would confuse passing ships.

Recipe of the week

CHILLI PORK BURGERS WITH STIR-FRIED CABBAGE

SERVES: 2
PREP: 10 mins
COOK: 15 mins

225g (8oz) lean pork fillet/tenderloin (all fat removed)
1 small onion, diced
1 garlic clove, crushed
1 red chilli, deseeded and diced
1 stalk lemongrass, peeled and finely sliced
1 tsp nam pla (Thai fish sauce)
A handful of coriander, finely chopped
Salt and freshly ground black pepper
Lime wedges to serve
Spray oil
1 tsp black mustard seeds
2cm fresh root ginger, peeled and diced
300g (10oz) Savoy or any dark green cabbage, roughly shredded
2 tbsp 0 per cent fat Greek yogurt

1 Blitz the pork, onion, garlic, chilli, lemongrass, nam pla and coriander in a food processor. Season with a little salt and pepper.
2 Divide the mixture into 4 portions, and mould each one into a burger.
3 Cook the burgers under a pre-heated hot grill for about 6–8 mins each side, until golden brown and the pork is cooked right through and is no longer pink.
4 Meanwhile, lightly spray a wok or deep frying pan with oil and cook the mustard seeds and ginger for 1 min until the seeds release their aroma.
5 Add the cabbage and stir-fry for 2-3 mins until it's slightly tender but still crisp. Take the pan off the heat and stir in the yogurt.
6 Serve immediately with the burgers and the lime wedges.
one2onediet.com

22 SUNDAY

23 MONDAY

24 TUESDAY

25 WEDNESDAY

26 THURSDAY

27 FRIDAY

28 SATURDAY

Down memory lane

A CARIBBEAN IDYLL

In 1953, when I was 12, my father, a sergeant in the army, was posted to Kingston, Jamaica. My mother and I went with him and moved into very nice married quarters with banana trees and exotic plants in the garden. We had our own maid, Katy, and a gardener, Cassie, who were both great characters.

The heat was a bit of a challenge at first, but we soon got used to it. We missed our family, of course, but we kept in touch by airmail and once we posted a coconut to my cousin with stamps on it like a parcel! We had a great social life. I joined the church choir and I used to meet my friends at the swimming pool on the camp. Going to the 'Carib' cinema was a special treat.

My mum and I used to go to the local markets on the bus in the company of Jamaican ladies with chickens on their laps and baskets on their heads. The two years we spent there were a wonderful experience. We were sad to leave behind our Alsatian, Kim, though we did find him a nice new home.
Pauline Johnson, Beverley

Name that tune

The last big hit for the singer with the dark sunglasses. plaintive high voice and brilliant growl, this song was used in a movie of the same name starring Julia Roberts and Richard Gere.

A: Pretty Woman, Roy Orbison

Word of the week
Collywobbles
It may be fun to say, however the meaning of collywobbles isn't quite so jolly. According to the Collins Dictionary, if something gives you the 'collywobbles' it gives you an upset stomach. It's thought to be derived from cholera morbus – the 'blue death' disease we now know as cholera.

Try something new!
Pen your own poem. A good way to start is by thinking of an event that has really inspired you, or on an occasion where you've felt strong emotions.

Uncommon knowledge

In Bringing Up Baby (1938), Cary Grant's character is roped into doing just that by Susan Vance, wonderfully portrayed by Katharine Hepburn.

Grant was afraid of the tame leopard, something Hepburn would take advantage of. Often finding it hilarious to throw a toy leopard into his dressing room.

Recipe of the week

EASY ASPARAGUS & RICOTTA PIZZAS

SERVES: 4
PREP: 20 mins
COOK: 15 mins

500g (1lb 1oz) Waitrose Sun-Dried Tomato & Chilli Bread Mix
250g (9oz) tub Italian Ricotta
230g (8oz) bunch British Asparagus, halved lengthways
1 tbsp olive oil
4 tbsp fresh Waitrose Green Pesto with Basil

1 Place the bread mix in a large bowl, setting aside a handful for dusting the surface. Make a well in the centre, add 250ml (8fl oz) lukewarm water then bring together to make a slightly sticky dough.
2 Knead the dough vigorously for 5 mins until it becomes smooth and elastic. Divide the dough into 4 even-sized balls then roll out to make 26 x 12cm (10x5in) ovals. Transfer to 2 large, non-stick baking sheets.
3 Pre-heat the oven to 220°C/ Fan 200°C /Gas Mark 7. Spoon the ricotta onto the pizza bases then place the asparagus on top. Drizzle lightly with olive oil and leave to rise for 10 mins.
4 Bake for 15 mins until the base is cooked through and the asparagus is tender. Dot over the pesto and finish with a good grinding of black pepper. Serve warm.
Waitrose.com

29 SUNDAY

30 MONDAY

31 TUESDAY

1 WEDNESDAY

2 THURSDAY

3 FRIDAY

4 SATURDAY

Down memory lane

GOD SAVE THE QUEEN

Like many families in the Fifties we did not own a car, a telephone or a television. On the morning of the Queen's Coronation on June 2, 1953, my mum and dad, my brother Allen, our dog Lassie and I set off across the fields to my Auntie Carrie's house to watch the ceremony on her TV. Squeezed up close on her brown moquette three-piece, our eyes were glued to the set, not wishing to miss a minute of this royal event.

One month later, Allen and I were ecstatic to be boarding the train from Leeds to London with our parents. As the fields sped by we played I Spy and spotted rabbits. We stayed with Mum's sister, Auntie Emmie, who lived near Watford and I shared a bed with my cousin Sylvia. The next morning we journeyed to the capital where we craned our necks looking up at the gigantic metal crowns and flags along The Mall. We could almost hear the cheering crowds who had lined the route four weeks before. Dad took this photo of Mum with me and Allen perched on a lion's giant paw in Trafalgar Square.

Margaret Humphries, Pudsey

Name that tune

'A-wop-bop-a-loo-mop' sounded like gobbledegook until an iconic rock 'n' roller made it into the catchiest of phrases that drove us all crazy in his deliciously 'sweet' song that changed music history in 1955.

A: *Tutti Frutti, Little Richard*

Word of the week
Zwodder
Meaning a 'drowsy and stupid state of body or mind' we've all felt in a bit of a zwodder at some stage in our lives – particularly when in need of a caffeine pick-me-up. It's thought to be a dialect word from the southeast of England and was particularly common in Somerset.

Try something new!
Go stone skimming. Find a still or calm body of water and choose flat stones that aren't too tiny or too large. With your thumb and first finger out, rest the stone on your second finger and try to spin it away from you in a straight flat line towards the water.

Uncommon knowledge

Bedknobs and Broomsticks (1971) was originally due for release in the Sixties, but Disney shelved it in favour of Mary Poppins. The Beautiful Briny Sea was originally written for Mary Poppins before being dropped. It was Angela Lansbury's first outing for Disney.

Recipe of the week

SIRLOIN STEAK & ROASTED TOMATO SALAD

SERVES: 2
PREP: 10 mins
COOK: 15 mins

160g (5½ oz) cherry tomatoes
1 tsp toasted sesame oil
1 tsp soy sauce
200g (7oz) green beans, trimmed
2 x 150g (5oz) sirloin steaks, trimmed of excess fat
1 tsp sunflower or olive oil
½ x 130g (4½ oz) pack Waitrose Watercress, Rocket & Spinach Salad
2 tbsp Waitrose Soy, Ginger & Chilli Dressing
1 tsp wasabi paste

1 Pre-heat the oven to 220°C/ Fan 200°C/Gas Mark 7. Toss the tomatoes with the sesame oil and soy in a small roasting tin. Roast for 15 mins, shaking the tin gently halfway. Meanwhile, simmer the beans in a pan of boiling water for 5 mins, then drain and rinse under cold water to cool; pat dry.
2 Heat a frying pan over a high heat. Brush the steaks with the sunflower (or olive) oil, season and fry for 1½ mins on each side, ensuring the cut surfaces are thoroughly cooked, then set aside to rest for 1 min.
3 Divide the salad between two plates and top with the tomatoes, sliced steak and beans. Mix the dressing with the wasabi paste, any steak resting juices and any cooking juices from the tomatoes; spoon over the top and serve.
waitrose.com

5 SUNDAY

6 MONDAY

7 TUESDAY

8 WEDNESDAY

9 THURSDAY

10 FRIDAY

11 SATURDAY

Down memory lane

THREE GIDDY GOATS

This is me with my mum and our goats which we acquired when my father did an exchange of goods with some travellers who had no cash. Dad decided to accept the goats as payment as we had a large garden which he hated mowing. We christened the nanny Mayday and her two kids were Pepsi and Cola.

The goats were cute but they were also trouble, rubbing the bark off our apple trees and often escaping. Mayday once managed to drag Mum along the ground by the tether when she was trying to milk her. One day we were having a tea party in the house when the goats came in through the open front door and crashed around, knocking things over. When I chased them out of one door they came back in through another door. It was like a Benny Hill sketch.

Soon after this incident my parents decided it was time for the goats to go. It was a case of history repeating itself as some people who came to mend our tin roof agreed to accept the goats as payment instead of cash!

Rose Janes, via email

Name that tune

A monkey playing drums in a TV advert reminded us how great this song was, but it was originally written about the divorce of the performer who had just left a 'biblically' huge band.

A: In the Air Tonight, Phil Collins

Word of the week

Eucatastrophe

Describing the sudden and favourable resolution of events in a story – in other words a happy twist to a tale or a happy ending. Coined by JRR Tolkien, who before becoming the writer we know today, worked as an assistant on the first edition of the Oxford English Dictionary.

Try something new!

Try a new look. Take a chance on an item of clothing you really like but isn't the sort of thing you normally wear, or let a partner or friend choose a new outfit for you! Ask your hairdresser to style your hair differently or just pick a new shade of lipstick.

Uncommon knowledge

Prince Charles and Princess Anne visited the set of popular children's programme, and forerunner to Blue Peter, Studio E. There they met none other than David Attenborough and Cocky the Cockatoo. A fantastic photo from 1958.

Recipe of the week

CHOCOLATE CHUNK COOKIES

MAKES: 10 Cookies
PREP: 10 mins
COOK: 12 mins

300g (10oz) plain flour
½ tsp bicarbonate of soda
120g (4oz) salted butter (melted)
225g (8oz) light brown soft sugar
1 egg
20 squares of milk chocolate

1 Pre-heat your oven to 180°C/Fan 160°C/Gas Mark 4.
2 In the mixing bowl, combine the flour and bicarbonate. Set to one side.
3 In the other bowl, add the melted butter and mix in the sugar before adding the egg. Add this wet mix to the dry flour mix and bring together with the wooden spoon to form a dough.
4 Divide the dough into 60g (2oz) balls and place on the lined baking tray, leaving room to spread between each one. Push each ball down slightly then place in the oven for 6 mins.
5 After the 6 mins, take the cookies out of the oven, press 2 squares of chocolate into each one, rotate the tray then bake for a further 6 mins.
6 Allow to cool slightly on the tray before serving.
Easy Peasy Baking fabflour.co.uk

12 SUNDAY

13 MONDAY

14 TUESDAY

15 WEDNESDAY

16 THURSDAY

17 FRIDAY

18 SATURDAY

Down memory lane

OUR SECRET ROMANCE

I first met Ray when I was 12 and he was 14. We were good friends, but by the time I was 15 we knew it was more than that. However, my parents thought I was too young for a serious relationship.

Ray and I decided to write to each other so we found a good post box just near a farm where I lived - it was a tree with a cavity in its trunk. All was fine until one day my brother and cousins climbed the tree and found one of our letters. My parents were not impressed! Our next hiding place was a loose brick in our front garden wall.

When I went away for a week to stay with a friend, Ray presented me with a large box before I boarded the train. It was an Oxo tin filled with red artificial roses and some lovely poems. He went away to college and we wrote to each other every day. We were engaged when I was 19 and wed two years later. We have been happily married for more than 52 years and I still have the letters he posted in the tree!
Merle Birch, High Wycombe

Name that tune

Someone clearly thought this song was all about them and yet great mystery still remains to this day as to who the subject of this deadly sins song of 1972 really is.

A: You're so Vain, Carly Simon

Word of the week

Flibbertigibbet

With onomatopoeic origins, flibbertigibbet is thought to come from the Middle English word flepergebet which means a gossip or chatterer. It now refers to a person with flighty and silly tendencies. The word appears in many tales including William Shakespeare's King Lear and in Sir Walter Scott's Kenilworth.

Try something new!

Write a gratitude list. Good things can often go unnoticed and it's a great way of becoming more aware and then passing on the gratitude. Each day for one week, write down a minimum of three things for which you're grateful. It can be about people, things, experiences. Whatever is happening in your life that sparks gratitude, big or small.

Uncommon knowledge

Debbie Reynolds was one of the few women invited to The Rat Pack's parties, as she was good friends with Frank Sinatra.

"When we worked together on The Tender Trap I was engaged to marry Eddie Fisher and Frank took me to lunch and said: 'Sweetie, don't get married. Don't marry a singer. We're nice guys but we're not good husbands.'" Eddie Fisher would later leave Reynolds for Elizabeth Taylor.

Recipe of the week

SALMON RAINBOW SALAD BOWL

SERVES: 2
PREP: 20 mins
COOK: 40 mins

2 tbsp turmeric
2 tbsp rapeseed oil
8 stems of purple sprouting broccoli
8 cauliflower florets
8 new/baby potatoes
2 red peppers, sliced
2 salmon fillets
2 handfuls of watercress or rocket
For the dressing:
3 tbsp low-fat yogurt
2 tsp rapeseed oil
2 tsp lemon juice
Zest of a lemon
1 tbsp fresh tarragon, finely chopped
Salt and black pepper to season

1 Pre-heat the oven to 200°C/Fan 180°C/Gas Mark 6.
2 Mix the turmeric and oil together. Place the broccoli and cauliflower onto a roasting dish, drizzle with 1 tbsp of the turmeric oil and roast for 10-15 mins. Add the red pepper and roast for another 10 mins until tender.
3 Wash the potatoes and simmer gently in salted water for around 10-15 mins until they're tender and cooked through. Remove from heat, drain and cut into bite-sized chunks.
5 Meanwhile place the salmon fillets onto a roasting tin, spread with the remaining turmeric mix, season and roast for 15 mins, until cooked through.
6 Mix all the ingredients for the dressing together in a large bowl. Once the potatoes, broccoli and cauliflower have cooled, place them into the bowl with the dressing and watercress.

seasonalspuds.com

19 SUNDAY

20 MONDAY

21 TUESDAY

22 WEDNESDAY

23 THURSDAY

24 FRIDAY

25 SATURDAY

Down memory lane

MY MAKE-BELIEVE WORLD

Here I am, happily playing in the garden of my family's two-up, two-down weatherboard house. I was the youngest of four, but my siblings were many years older and as we lived on a main road there were no other children to play with so I was left to make my own amusement.

We had a small shed which I made into my little house with a crate for a table on which I spread my china tea set. Dolls were sat around the table with their plates of untouched food; stones were potatoes, leaves for vegetables and bits of wood for meat. Mud pies were the puddings (a little messy, needless to say). When I was eight I started making my dolls' clothes, buying little pieces of pretty cotton fabric. Mum bought me a toy sewing machine, but I found sewing by hand was easier.

Every Friday Dad gave me sixpence pocket money. I used this to buy a book when out shopping with Mum. I read all the Famous Five and Secret Seven books by Enid Blyton and used to get completely lost in the stories.
Evelyn Downs, via email

Name that tune

We just can't get this song out of our heads. First recorded by Gwen McCrae, and later covered by the Pet Shop Boys, its Seventies release by singing royalty is how it's best known.

A: Always on My Mind, Elvis Presley

Word of the week

Snickersnee

Sounds quite jolly doesn't it? Actually, the meaning is a little dark. Snickersnee is a large sword-like knife used as a weapon for cutting, or refers to fighting with knives.

Try something new!

Take yourself on a solo date. Whether it be a stroll in the park with ice-cream, tucking into a portion of fish and chips at the seaside or a quiet evening with your favourite drink or TV show. Whatever it is, doing something for yourself is a great way to practice self-care.

Uncommon knowledge

Relationships blossomed with the all-star cast of Clash of the Titans. Dame Maggie Smith, married to producer Beverley Cross, helped convince her friend Sir Laurence Olivier to join the crew. Perseus himself, Harry Hamlin, had a child with Ursula Andress during production.

Recipe of the week

CARBONARA-STYLE SPAGHETTI IN THE MICROWAVE

SERVES: 2
PREP: 5 mins
COOK: 9 mins

100g (4oz) spaghetti
50g (2oz) frozen peas
4 rashers of smoked back bacon
3 large British Lion eggs
100ml/4floz single cream
25g (1oz) freshly grated Parmesan cheese
A little grated nutmeg
Salt and freshly ground black pepper

1 Boil a kettle of water. Snap the spaghetti in half and place it in the bowl. Pour over enough boiling water from the kettle to fill half the bowl, cover with an upturned plate. Cook on high for 7 mins. Stir in the peas and leave to stand for 2 mins.
2 Chop the bacon and put in a small micro-proof bowl, cover with a piece of kitchen paper to prevent splattering, and cook on high for 1 min 30 secs, stirring once. Transfer to a plate and set aside.
3 Beat the eggs, cream and cheese together with the nutmeg and seasoning. Drain the pasta in a colander, return it to the bowl, stir in the bacon, and egg mixture. Cook on high for 2 mins, stirring once. Leave to stand for 2 mins. Serve in bowls with a little more nutmeg grated and ground pepper over the top.

British Lion Eggs eggrecipes.co.uk

26 SUNDAY

27 MONDAY

28 TUESDAY

29 WEDNESDAY

30 THURSDAY

1 FRIDAY

2 SATURDAY

Down memory lane

LIFE ON THE MOVE

This is me (on the left) with my parents and little sister outside the caravan we called home from 1943 to 1952. Dad worked in forestry so we travelled around Yorkshire. There was a bedroom at each end and a living area in the middle. It had a wood-burning stove, a Belfast sink and a tap that could be connected to a water supply. For washdays Mum had the old tub and peggy which must have been jolly hard work.

Sixty years later, my brother and sister and I decided to find the caravan for old times' sake. We tracked it down to a vehicle reclamation yard, looking somewhat dilapidated as the picture shows. The owner's son told us they planned to reuse the chassis, wheels and roof so, happily, its life was not over yet.
Norah Rudge, Stroud

Name that tune

It's the longest single-word title to appear in a UK chart-topper but that hasn't stopped it being sung in almost every house for special occasions. It came second in the 1968 Eurovision song contest.

A: Congratulations, Cliff Richard

Word of the week
Poppycock
While this slang word sounds distinctly British, it has American origins and can be traced as far back as 1852. There are a few possible roots for this humorous sounding word, but one rather odd theory includes the Dutch word for doll 'pap' and 'cack', which means excrement.

Try something new!
Rearrange your furniture. Change your space by moving your bed, sofa or table to a different part of a room. If you can't get help with the lifting, try changing the placement of smaller decorative items, such as photo frames, mirrors, rugs and ornaments.

Uncommon knowledge

It was the legendary concept artist Ralph McQuarrie who first suggested that Darth Vader should have a breathing apparatus. McQuarrie took inspiration from breath masks and samurai helms to create Vader's iconic visage.

Recipe of the week

CHORIZO & RED PEPPER CIABATTA ROLLS

SERVES: 4
PREP: 15 mins
COOK: 20 mins

4 ciabatta rolls
2 red peppers
1 tbsp olive oil
1 garlic clove, crushed
Salt and black pepper
200g (7oz) pack Unearthed Smoked Cooking Chorizo
4 tbsp aioli (garlic mayonnaise)
½ lemon, zest and juice
45g (1½ oz) pack wild rocket

1 Pre-heat the oven to 200°C/ Fan 180°C /Gas Mark 6, put the rolls on a baking tray and bake for 10 mins. Meanwhile, set a large griddle over a medium-high heat. Slice down and around the peppers to cut off the 'cheeks' (leaving just the stalk and a little pepper at the base which can be saved for salads). Toss with the oil and garlic, season and griddle for 5 mins on each side.
2 Taking care not to slice completely through the skin, cut lengthways through the chorizo sausages. Flatten with the base of your hand and cook on the griddle for 5-6 mins on each side. Mix the aioli with the lemon zest and a good grinding of black pepper.
3 Split open the ciabatta rolls and spread one side of each with some aioli. Fill each with a split chorizo sausage, 2 pieces of red pepper and a handful of rocket; give each a final spritz of lemon juice before serving.

waitrose.com

3 SUNDAY

4 MONDAY

5 TUESDAY

6 WEDNESDAY

7 THURSDAY

8 FRIDAY

9 SATURDAY

Down memory lane

THE MARYLEBONE GIRLS

This photo is a celebration of friendship. It shows my wonderful group of friends called The Marylebone Girls because we were all born in that part of London in 1946. We went to the same school and did many other things together including being confirmed at our local church and going to the youth club where we did a lot of dancing! In the holidays, we were out all day at the park or swimming.

We share so many memories. We've had children, in some cases within weeks of each other, and remained steadfast through marriages and sometimes divorces. We have been through family losses and always been there for each other.

Over the years we have met up regularly to have lunch and several glasses of wine. Our conversations are about life in general, but we still enjoy remembering the things we got up to as youngsters, some of which were quite naughty. We were the generation that bunked off school to hop on a bus and go out for the day!
Eileen Trotter via email

Name that tune

Named after a sartorial icon, this song inspired a whole following of its own and even a totally new style of dance. Ginger Rogers, Lauren Bacall and Marlon Brando all played their part in the track.

A: Vogue, Madonna

Word of the week

Boondoggle

Meaning an extravagant or useless project, boondoggle is also a name for plaited accessories made popular by the Scouts. Boondoggles hit US headlines in 1935 when the New York Times claimed more than $3 million had been spent on teaching the unemployed useless craft skills including the making of boondoggles!

Try something new!

Attend a dance class. From ballroom to ballet, enter your postcode on finddanceclasses.co.uk to find out what's on near you. If you feel a little nervous, try a virtual class in the comfort of your own home via YouTube, or simply get up and dance to some of your favourite tunes in the kitchen!

Uncommon knowledge

Dad's Army was one of a handful of TV shows to see out the change from black and white to colour television. Having been broadcast in both, Ian Lavender, who played the dopey character Pike made a bold claim: "[I was] the first actor to be killed by a colour TV set on colour TV in Z Cars when a robbery went wrong and the TV set was dropped on me from a great height by Nicholas Jones."

Recipe of the week

SUMMER BERRY CHOCOLATE TRAYBAKE

SERVES: 12
PREP: 10 mins
COOK: 25-30 mins

175g (6oz) self-raising flour
150g (5oz) light brown sugar
50g (2oz) cocoa powder
1 tsp bicarbonate of soda
150ml (5 floz) milk
2 eggs
150ml oil (5 floz) (vegetable or sunflower)
450ml (15floz) double cream
Strawberries, blueberries, raspberries or cherries

1 Pre-heat the oven to 180°C/Fan 160°C/Gas Mark 4 and line the traybake tin with baking parchment.
2 In the mixing bowl, fully combine the flour, sugar, cocoa powder and bicarbonate with the whisk before adding the milk, eggs and oil.
3 Mix everything together to form a smooth batter, then pour into the lined traybake tin. Place in the oven on the middle shelf and bake for 25-30 mins until springy in the centre.
4 Allow the sponge to cool before removing from the tin.
5 Whip the cream to soft peaks, swirl on top of the cooled sponge and top with your preferred berries just before serving.

Easy Peasy Baking fabflour.co.uk

10 SUNDAY

11 MONDAY

12 TUESDAY

13 WEDNESDAY

14 THURSDAY

15 FRIDAY

16 SATURDAY

Down memory lane

A SUMMER IN SCOTLAND

I feel so proud of this photo taken in the summer of 1951. My dad, Ken, was a teacher and during the long summer holidays he used to go away on courses as a Sea Cadet officer. On this particular year he went to Arbroath in Scotland.

We followed, travelling on the sleeper train to Edinburgh. Great excitement for us children, but a lot of work for Mum with sewing and mending and having to pack for us all. We stayed in a guest house run by a Mrs Phillips where I remember my little brother got his head stuck between the banisters on the landing.

This picture of our family was taken when we joined the sea cadets on a trip to Dundee. My overriding memory of the experience is of great freedom, being able to run around and pick wild flowers. Marjory, my mum, was always so smart. She had shiny, chestnut hair which she styled beautifully herself. I am standing next to her, my sister Janet is in front of Dad who is holding young Philip, looking none the worse for his banister ordeal!
Susan Willett, Hythe

Name that tune

The lyrics were inspired by Janis Joplin, but this song was actually performed in tribute to a different tragic star. It was later rewritten after the untimely death of a public figure in 1997.

A: Candle in the Wind, Elton John

Word of the week
Gaberlunzie
A medieval Scots word for licensed beggar, gaberlunzie has appeared in the books of several distinguished novelists including Sir Walter Scott, Thomas Hardy and Patrick O'Brian. More recently it had an airing in season one of the popular TV series Outlander.

Try something new!
Capture a moment of your day with a photo. It can be anything - like a bird perched on the garden fence, a tasty homemade meal you've prepared, a pretty flower on an afternoon stroll, or a beautiful sunset.

Uncommon knowledge

Glenn Ford takes on a devious crime syndicate in The Big Heat, with Jocelyn Brando, Marlon's older sister also appearing. As their damsel, Columbia originally wanted Marilyn Monroe, but her fee was too high so instead cast the glorious Gloria Grahame.

Recipe of the week

CHERRY, MASCARPONE & AMARETTI POTS

SERVES: 4
PREP: 20 mins
COOK: None

180g (6oz) pack Waitrose & Partners Cherries
2 tbsp icing sugar
1 tbsp lemon juice
150g (5oz) mascarpone
150g (5oz) natural yogurt
½ tsp vanilla bean paste
100g (4oz) amaretti biscuits

1 Halve and stone the cherries, then toss in a bowl with 1 tbsp icing sugar and the lemon juice, and set aside for 15 mins, stirring occasionally.
2 In a bowl, mix the mascarpone, yogurt, remaining 1 tbsp icing sugar and vanilla paste. Put the amaretti biscuits in a clean food bag and crush into rough pieces with a rolling pin.
3 Divide ½ the crushed biscuits between 4 wine glasses, tumblers or jam jars. Divide ½ the mascarpone mixture between the glasses, layering it over the biscuits, then top with ½ the macerated cherries. Repeat to create a second layer. Serve immediately or make up to 2 hours in advance, chilling until ready to serve.
Waitrose.com

17 SUNDAY

18 MONDAY

19 TUESDAY

20 WEDNESDAY

21 THURSDAY

22 FRIDAY

23 SATURDAY

Down memory lane

SHELTERED FROM DANGER

Having been born in 1941, I have a few memories of the war. A very vivid one is of someone, presumably my dad, carrying me in his arms and running from the house to the air raid shelter in our garden. It was dark and I was wrapped in a blanket. I can still see arms reaching up to take me as I was handed down to Mum or maybe Gran.

Dad had built our shelter by digging a huge hole in the lawn before burying the shelter deep in the ground with a few steps leading down into it. It was quite snug, with a couple of narrow bunks along one side and a chair at the end where Gran used to sit. I remember looking up at the silhouette of my dad sitting in the entrance, watching the night sky as enemy planes droned overhead.

One night we had a lucky escape as a low-flying plane released a bomb which bounced in the road outside our house before exploding two streets away. On VE Day my brother Billy and I watched from our bedroom window as the neighbours built a bonfire in the crater it had left.
Carole Bryan, Theydon Bois

Name that tune

The biggest UK hit for an unconventional and hugely colourful Eighties boy band all about the freedom to be yourself, this song reminded us that a reptile believes what goes around comes around.

A: Karma Chameleon, Culture Club

Word of the week

Sandwich

This picnic favourite is thought to be named after the 4th Earl of Sandwich, who was very particular about the foods he ate while playing cards. One day he ordered 'some meat tucked between two slices of bread' which meant he could keep his fingers clean while he played.

Try something new!

Watch a movie you've never seen before by yourself. Pick up a DVD from a charity shop or take advantage of a free trial with a streaming service like Netflix or Amazon Video.

Uncommon knowledge

Derek Meddings helped pioneer the "supermarionation" technique alongside Gerry Anderson for Thunderbirds, and his many other marionette programmes. Meddings would take the miniature techniques he developed and use them on many other films, including James Bond.

Recipe of the week

ASIAN TUNA RAINBOW BOWL

SERVES: 2
PREP: 5 mins
COOK: 12 mins

Half a mug brown rice
1 tbsp honey
1 tbsp soy sauce
½ tbsp sesame oil
1 large carrot, cut into ribbons
6 radishes, thinly sliced
2 x 110g cans Princes Drained Tuna Steak in Spring Water
1 handful of frozen edamame beans, thawed
100g (4oz) sweetcorn, drained
Sprinkle of sesame seeds

1 Add the rice along with 1 mug of water to a saucepan with a lid and cook over a medium heat for about 12 mins until all the water is absorbed and the rice is cooked. Allow to cool.
2 To make the sauce, mix together the honey, soy and sesame oil.
3 Cut the carrot into ribbons using a potato peeler and slice the radishes into thin slices.
4 Pack the rice into a tea cup, ramekin or small bowl and turn it out onto the middle of your serving bowl to create a domed effect, repeat with second bowl.
5 Pile the tuna, carrot ribbons, edamame beans, sliced radishes and sweetcorn around the edges of the bowls. Drizzle over the sauce and sprinkle with sesame seeds.

Miguel Barclay/Princes, princes.co.uk

24 SUNDAY

25 MONDAY

26 TUESDAY

27 WEDNESDAY

28 THURSDAY

29 FRIDAY

30 SATURDAY

Down memory lane

OUR PERFECT PREFAB

My mum and dad met when they were in the army during the war and married just before it ended. In 1949, they were given the tenancy of a new prefab in New Inn, Pontypool. My mum watched the prefabs being put up, not knowing that one of them would be their home. I was born in our prefab and it is where my sister and I grew up and had a lovely childhood.

It had good-sized rooms with an open fire and lots of cupboards for storage. We had a nice big garden where Dad grew all his vegetables. Mum had a fridge and a boiler in which to do the washing.

When I was 15, the prefabs were demolished and replaced by new houses. We moved in to one of the houses, but we were sad because we had a lot of happy memories of our first home. However, there is an identical prefab at St Fagan's Museum in Cardiff that we can always go to see when we want to remember our childhood days.

Dorothy Thomas, Raglan

Name that tune

You know the dance moves that were made up by crowds watching an episode of American Bandstand in 1979. The tune from this 'capital' band has been picking us off the ground at discos ever since.

A: YMCA, The Village People

Word of the week

Honorificabilitudinitatibus

The longest word in the English language that features alternating consonants and vowels, it means the state of being able to achieve honours. It's also the longest word to appear in the works by William Shakespeare and no doubt filled stage actors with dread!

Try something new!

Strike up a conversation with a stranger or someone you've never talked to before - this could be in a queue at a supermarket, on a park bench or in a friendly online community, such as the **Yours** Meeting Place forum. Visit facebook.com/groups/YoursMeetingPlace

Uncommon knowledge

In Gremlins, there is no furry monster worse than Spike, the polar opposite of the cute Gizmo. Spike's snarls were in fact voiced by none other than legendary voice actor Frank Welker, who also gave voice to Fred from Scooby Doo, as well as Curious George and Garfield!

Recipe of the week

LEMON TART

SERVES: 6
PREP: 5 mins
COOK: 20 mins

3 large British Lion eggs
1 x 20cm (8in) ready-baked sweet pastry case
75g (3oz) caster sugar
1 x 200g (7oz) tub crème fraîche
Zest and juice of 2 lemon
Icing sugar to dust
Clotted cream to serve

1 Pre-heat the oven to 170°C/Fan 150°C/Gas Mark 3. Place the pastry case on a baking sheet. Beat the eggs, sugar, crème fraîche, lemon zest and juice together until smooth.
2 Pour the mixture into the pastry case. Bake for 25-30 mins or until the filling is just set, but still a little wobbly in the centre. Cool. Chill for at least 2 hours.
3 Dust with icing sugar and serve in wedges with clotted cream.

British Lion Eggs eggrecipes.co.uk

31 SUNDAY

1 MONDAY

2 TUESDAY

3 WEDNESDAY

4 THURSDAY

5 FRIDAY

6 SATURDAY

Down memory lane

A CHINA DOG STORY

The photo shows me as Brown Owl (on the left in the back row) with my Brownie pack at Greenford in London. On my wedding in August 1969 Sandra (third from left in the middle row) came up to me and handed me a package, saying 'This is for you'. When I arrived back from my honeymoon I opened the package to find a china dog.

The years passed and my husband and I moved to Harefield in Middlesex. One day, on my way back to work after lunch, I noticed a woman carrying a child and struggling to fold up a pushchair. I asked if she needed assistance and she looked up at me and said: "Hello, Captain." It was Sandra! We only had time to say a few words before the bus came and I helped her on board. I never had time to ask her what she was doing in Harefield. I wish we'd been able to talk. I could have told her that the china dog has moved with us seven times since we got married and he now sits in my guest bedroom.

June Jones, Ashley Heath

Name that tune

Originally influenced by Eleanor Roosevelt, the song was later renamed for an Anne Bancroft film that only missed out on a best song Oscar because the band forgot to fill out the nomination forms.

A: Mrs Robinson, Simon and Garfunkel

Word of the week

Ragamuffin

Ragamuffin's first literary use was in its original spelling of ragamoffynm, as a name for Satan in William Langland's poem Piers Plowman. Today's meaning has softened and is often used to describe a lovable rogue or a person in tatty clothes.

Try something new!

Reconnect with an old friend. Send them a letter, message them on social media or give them a call. You'll be glad you did!

Uncommon knowledge

Not much of a glorious feeling on the set of Singin' in the Rain, with the numerous injuries suffered by the stars. Donald O'Connor was hospitalised after the somersaults he performed in Make 'Em Laugh, Debbie Reynolds had burst blood vessels in her feet after Good Morning and Gene Kelly suffered from a fever when filming the iconic Singin' in the Rain number.

Recipe of the week

STRAWBERRY MALLOW MOUSSE

SERVES: 6
PREP: 15 mins (+ 6 hours to set)
COOK: None

400g (14oz) pack essential Waitrose British Strawberries
Grated zest and juice 1 orange
40g (1½ oz) caster sugar
250g (8oz) mini white marshmallows
2 x 200g (7oz) tubs Waitrose Fromage Frais
2 tbsp roughly chopped pistachios

1 Reserve 6 small strawberries for decoration. Hull and roughly chop the rest and put them in a saucepan with the orange zest and juice, plus sugar. Stir over a gentle heat until the sugar has dissolved, then simmer for 5-10 mins until the strawberries are soft and pulpy.
2 Mash with a fork and stir in the marshmallows until melted. Transfer to a bowl and set aside to cool.
3 Fold the fromage frais into the strawberry mixture and spoon into 6 serving glasses. Chill for at least 6 hours, until set.
4 Hull and slice the reserved strawberries and arrange on top of the mousses. Scatter over the pistachios to serve.
waitrose.com

7 SUNDAY

8 MONDAY

9 TUESDAY

10 WEDNESDAY

11 THURSDAY

12 FRIDAY

13 SATURDAY

Down memory lane

A FAMILY MAN

This photo of my dad was taken on the beach at Worthing in 1970. He was a quiet, kind man and good company with a dry sense of humour. His family was his life.

Mum was a teacher and spent time on Sundays dealing with school work so Dad would take me and my two sisters on a jaunt in his light blue Morris Minor. He was an avid walker so a favourite trip was to the Peak District, a half hour drive from our home in Oldham. Years before walking became really popular we were traversing Chew brook which flows into Dovestone reservoir. Occasionally Dad would guide us all up nearby Indians Head hill which is 1,000 feet high – and we would still be back home in time for dinner at two.

Dad was also a keen swimmer and taught me to swim at the local swimming baths. I achieved my length certificate when I was eight. Sadly, he died of a heart attack aged 52, but his legacy lives on. I still enjoy walking in the countryside and when I'm on holiday I love to swim in the sea.
Julie Ebden, Prestwich

Name that tune

We have to feel in the right 'frame of mind' for this big band tune. Considered racy when released in 1939, a little bit is played at the end of All You Need is Love.

A: In the Mood, Glenn Miller

Word of the week

Bloviate

Meaning to speak a lot in an annoying way as if you're very important. This 19th Century American word was rarely used, but would be a very useful addition to our vocabulary today.

Try something new!

Walk 10,000 steps a day. Get hold of a pedometer or use an exercise tracking app on your smartphone, then reward yourself at the end of the week with your favourite treat.

Uncommon knowledge

Blood may be thicker than water, but oil is thicker than them both. None of the trials and tribulations at Southfork Ranch would ever come close to the mystery of Who Shot JR? Even The Simpsons parodied Dallas' landmark plotline. When Larry Hagman (JR Ewing) was on holiday in the UK, he was supposedly offered £100,000 to spill the beans.

Recipe of the week

FLATBREADS WITH TZATZIKI

SERVES: 6
PREP: 15 mins
COOK: 4 mins

200g (7oz) self-raising flour
½ tsp baking powder
200g (7oz) natural yogurt
100g (4oz) melted butter
1 tsp cumin seeds
For the dip:
100g (4oz) natural yogurt
50g (2oz) cucumber (grated)
1 tsp mint sauce

1 Combine the flour, baking powder and cumin seeds in the mixing bowl, then add the yoghurt and 30g (1oz) of the melted butter to form a dough.
2 Turn out the dough onto a floured surface and knead for a few mins.
3 Heat up your frying pan to a medium-high heat. Divide the dough into 6 equal portions and roll out into 15-20cm circles.
4 Place each one into the hot pan one at a time and cook for 2 mins on each side until slightly puffed and toasted. Rub them with the remaining melted butter and serve whole or sliced into strips for dipping.
5 To make the dip, grate the cucumber and squeeze out the excess liquid into the sink with your hands. Then place the grated cucumber into the serving bowl, add the yogurt and mint sauce and mix.

Easy Peasy Baking fabflour.co.uk

14 SUNDAY

15 MONDAY

16 TUESDAY

17 WEDNESDAY

18 THURSDAY

19 FRIDAY

20 SATURDAY

Down memory lane

WHITE SANDS AND COCONUT PALMS

In 1959 when I was 19 and newly married, I flew to Malaya to join my husband, John, who was in the RAF. I had never flown before and the journey took five days.

After six months we were posted to Singapore to join 209 Squadron at Seletar. We lived nearby at Serangoon in a three-bedroom bungalow with an amah (maid) who came daily to do the cleaning and washing. I did not like the heat, but we had a wonderful life with lots of coffee mornings and parties.

At the weekend one of our favourite things was to hire a sampan and sail out to a very small rocky island called Telekor. We would often spend the day there with friends, swimming and snorkelling. There were white sands and coconut palms swaying in a soft breeze. It was Paradise – who could want for more? All these years later, those two and a half years spent in Singapore with my late husband seem like a dream.
Carol Tarbox, Gloucester

Name that tune

Reportedly disliked by both its Canadian singer and the director of the 'monumental' 1997 movie for which it became famous, this award-winning song certainly didn't sink in the music charts.

A: My Heart Will Go On, Celine Dion

Word of the week

Clapperclaw

As the name suggests, clapperclaw has some relation to our favourite feline friends. To clapperclaw means to fight by scratching and clawing with your fingernails. Miaow!

Try something new!

Be spontaneous... take a different route home, make a snap decision and stick to it or put yourself in a new environment. Say 'yes' to invitations!

Uncommon knowledge

Queen of the Galaxy, Barbarella was a sci-fi hit, and has impacted pop culture for decades. Duran Duran took the inspiration for their name, unsurprisingly from the villain Dr Durand Durand. Jane Fonda would later hit the headlines with fitness videos and political activism that saw her infamously named, Hanoi Jane.

Recipe of the week

CIDER-SOAKED BBQ PORK KEBABS

SERVES: 4
PREP: 10 mins + marinating
COOK: 25 mins

½ a 568ml bottle Stella Artois Cidre
4 tbsp maple syrup
4 cloves garlic, halved
8 sprigs thyme
420g (14oz) pork fillet, cubed
2 courgettes, thickly sliced
8 shallots, halved
1 red pepper, seeded and thickly sliced
Olive oil spray

1 Place the cider in a large glass bowl and stir in 2 tbsp of the maple syrup, the garlic cloves and half the thyme sprigs. Add the pork and leave to soak for at least an hour or overnight.
2 Lift out the pork, discarding the marinade. Thread the meat and vegetables alternately onto 8 metal skewers. Spray lightly with the oil.
3 Barbecue, grill or griddle the skewers for 15–20 mins, turning regularly until cooked through.
4 Strip the leaves from the remaining thyme sprigs and stir into the remaining maple syrup. Brush onto the skewers and continue to cook for a further 5 mins until shiny and nicely browned. Serve with leafy salad and a chilled glass of the remaining cider.
Waitrose.com

21 SUNDAY

22 MONDAY

23 TUESDAY

24 WEDNESDAY

25 THURSDAY

26 FRIDAY

27 SATURDAY

Down memory lane

HAPPY DAYS AT HERNE BAY

This is a photo of my brother and me taken by our dad with his box Brownie camera. Every year we went on holiday to Herne Bay, travelling by steam train from Chatham. Our excitement rose as we saw the sea in the distance. Finally we arrived at our guesthouse where we enjoyed full board.

We soon fell into holiday mode. This meant playing on the pebble beach, looking for patches of sand with which to make puddeny pies topped with a paper flag. Mid-morning we went to the King's Hall where I always had a bottle of Orange Dew and a Penguin. Sometimes Dad would take us for a walk along the beach and we would find rock pools where we could look for baby crabs. The amusement arcade with its slot machines was a favourite haunt. For a treat we'd go to one of the ice-cream parlours and have a sundae.

All too soon it was time to pack up and go home. Mum had had a good rest and we had enjoyed playing. Our holiday was quite tame by today's standards, but we thought of it as an adventure.

Janet King, via email

Name that tune

Get ready to twirl those multicoloured skirts for one of the most famous and sparkling songs of the Eighties. That this tune was going to become a worldwide bit, well there was never any contest.

A: Making Your Mind Up, Bucks Fizz

Word of the week

Codswallop

There are many theories about the slang word codswallop. One such tale involves British fizzy drink maker Hiram Codd who patented the Codd-neck bottle. Wallop was a slang term for beer and Codd's wallop became a term of contempt to describe weak gassy ale housed in the bottles.

Try something new!

Attend a play or musical. Visit your local theatre for a timetable or events or use Google to find a drama society that run affordable shows.

Uncommon knowledge

"You will never find a more wretched hive of scum and villainy". From Jedi Knights to British Officers, Alec Guinness's illustrious career has cemented him as one of the greats. Sadly, he didn't hold himself in such high regard, commenting: "I am a fraud, a phoney and with a second-class talent."

Recipe of the week

SUMMER FRUIT TRIFLE

SERVES: 10
PREP: 25 mins (+ overnight setting)
COOK: None

12 trifle sponge fingers
200g (7oz) fresh strawberries, washed, destalked and quartered
2 sachets of strawberry flavour jelly crystals plus 285ml (10 fl oz) of hot water
3 tbsp maple syrup
300ml (10 fl oz) ready-made custard
125ml (4½ fl oz) whipping cream
125g (4½ oz) fresh blueberries
125g (4½ oz) fresh raspberries
100g (4oz) fresh blackberries

1 Break the sponge fingers into pieces and place in the base of the trifle dish. Scatter with a handful of strawberries.
2 Dissolve one sachet of jelly crystals in 285ml (10 fl oz) of boiling water and add the maple syrup. Pour over the sponge fingers and strawberries and leave to set overnight in the fridge.
3 Spread a layer of cold custard over the set jelly and strawberries and top with raspberries and blueberries and set aside - leave enough for topping.
4 Repeat the process for a second layer of jelly and fruit
5 In a separate bowl, whip the cream to form stiff peaks and generously spread a thick layer on top of the fruit
6 Decorate with the remaining strawberries, raspberries, blueberries and blackberries and chill to set before serving.
maplefromcanada.co.uk

28 SUNDAY

29 MONDAY

30 TUESDAY

31 WEDNESDAY

1 THURSDAY

2 FRIDAY

3 SATURDAY

Down memory lane

IT WAS THE SIXTIES!

I am on the left of this photo which was taken in 1968. My friend (who lived next door but one) and I were 14 and considered ourselves too grown up for childhood games. We were much more interested in listening to the latest pop records. I was desperate to have a record player so that I could buy the top 20 hits on vinyl, but there was no way my father was going to buy me one.

With great determination I saved all my wages from my Saturday job, plus my pocket money. I finally had enough to buy a portable Dansette so during the school holidays we set it up in the garden with an extension lead and power from the electric socket in my father's shed. We had our own free radio station!

Our favourite groups were The Love Affair, The Small Faces, Dave Dee, Dozy, Mick and Titch as well as The Monkees and Amen Corner. (We didn't rate The Beatles so much at that time.) Goodness knows what the neighbours thought – maybe they really enjoyed our playlist because they never complained!
Sue Holmes, via email

Name that tune

A Northamptonshire priest and Scottish pop star made up the band that covered this No 1 hit that became the best-selling single of 1986.

A: Don't Leave Me This Way, the Communards

Word of the week

Sonder

Sonder is the realisation that each random passer-by is living a life as vivid and complex as your own. Coined by US writer John Koenig, Sonder has become an Instagram favourite, yet it appears in the Collins English Dictionary with an altogether different meaning relating to small racing yachts.

Try something new!

Learn a new skill. Adult education centres and city colleges run beginner classes covering all manner of useful skills - from pottery and painting to photography and cookery.

Uncommon knowledge

Celebrating its 72nd birthday this month, Disney's first step into live-action cinema was full of pirate booty, in Treasure Island. Walt Disney had considered, before dismissing, including a short animated sequence named Reynard the Fox, the concept art of which would become Disney's Robin Hood.

Recipe of the week

CRUSTLESS TOMATO QUICHE

SERVES: 8
PREP: 15 mins
COOK: 1 hour

1 tbsp olive oil
125g (4½ oz) breadcrumbs
4 eggs
175ml (6fl oz) whole milk
2 tbsp maple syrup
2 carrots, peeled and grated
1 courgette, grated and squeezed to remove excess water
½ leek, thinly sliced
150g (5oz) mature Cheddar cheese, grated
Salt and pepper, for seasoning
8 cherry tomatoes, halved

1 Pre-heat oven to 180°C/ Fan 160°C/Gas Mark 4.
2 Lightly oil a 25cm round non-stick dish and coat with breadcrumbs. Set aside.
3 In a bowl, beat together eggs, milk, maple syrup and stir in the grated carrots, grated courgette and the sliced leeks.
4 Add in the grated cheese, season with salt and pepper and thoroughly stir together.
5 Pour mixture into the non-stick dish and scatter with cherry tomatoes.
6 Bake for 45-60 mins until the middle has set then allow the quiche to stand for 10 mins before serving. Serve with a green salad.

maplefromcanada.co.uk

4 SUNDAY

5 MONDAY

6 TUESDAY

7 WEDNESDAY

8 THURSDAY

9 FRIDAY

10 SATURDAY

Down memory lane

I WAS DADDY'S GIRL

This photo was taken of me, aged ten, with my foster father. We were on holiday on the Norfolk Broads and had taken a boat trip from Great Yarmouth. Mum suffered from travel sickness so it was Dad who took me on these excursions. We once went on a boat trip from Bristol to Cardiff docks just so I could say I had been to Wales even though we didn't disembark!

I was a daddy's girl and he was very protective of me. When I was older and wanted to go on a date with a friend's brother he gave his permission, but insisted that the boy should knock on the door and come in to be inspected before I was allowed to go in his car.

Dad was also very strict about the time I had to be home at night. Once, when I was considerably later than the time specified, I was greeted by a bobby standing at our front gate. Dad had called the police! To add to my embarrassment, this was on my 18th birthday. Now of course I realise he only did it because he really loved me.
Elaine Hicklin, Alvaston

Name that tune

This song was hardly the kiss of death for the girl from Tiger Bay for whom it became her biggest hit. Written for a film of the same name, it features an almighty final note.

A: Goldfinger, Shirley Bassey

Word of the week

Mollycoddle

To treat with indulgent care, or a pampered person, today we use the word mollycoddle in the sense that we might 'spoil' someone for the worst. It's thought to be derived from the word coddle, meaning to treat someone in an over-protective way.

Try something new!

Eat at a restaurant on your own. Find somewhere online that serves your favourite food and if you feel a little nervous, book a table in advance and ask to be seated in a private corner, or time your visit outside peak hours.

Uncommon knowledge

The Philadelphia Story (1940), a rom-com based on the Broadway show, scored the Best Actor Oscar for James Stewart. Katharine Hepburn had starred in the stage version previously and had been gifted the film rights. Cary Grant had demanded over $100,000 for his role, but donated the lot to support the British War Relief Fund.

Recipe of the week

CHUNKY FISH FINGER SANDWICHES

SERVES: 2
PREP: 10 mins
COOK: 15 mins

100g (4oz) fresh white breadcrumbs from 4 slices white bloomer bread
2 eggs
½ tsp salt
1 tbsp milk
2 tbsp plain flour
300g (10oz) skinless and boneless hake
4 tbsp Crisp 'n Dry
Handful salad leaves, cucumber slices, tartare sauce

1 Make the breadcrumbs by whizzing chunks of white bread in a food processor then tip the crumbs into a shallow bowl.
2 Crack the eggs into another shallow bowl, add the salt and milk and mix with a fork. Place the flour into a third shallow bowl.
3 Cut the hake into chunky fingers. Dip the fish first into the flour, then the egg mixture, then the breadcrumbs. Turn to coat well on all sides then set on a plate until they're all coated.
4 Heat 2 tbsp of the oil in a large non-stick frying pan over medium high heat and carefully add the fish fingers. Fry for 2-3 mins or so until starting to turn golden then turn over (you may need to drizzle another tablespoon of oil into the pan) and cook for a further 2-3 mins, depending on thickness.
5 Reduce the heat to medium and cook for a further 4 mins or so, turning halfway through.
6. Assemble sandwich and serve with tartare sauce.
Crisp 'n Dry crispndry.co.uk

11 SUNDAY

12 MONDAY

13 TUESDAY

14 WEDNESDAY

15 THURSDAY

16 FRIDAY

17 SATURDAY

Down memory lane

A LIKELY TALE, DAD!

This is me with my mum taken on board the Wingfield Castle, a paddle steamer that used to be based in Hull.

A recent television documentary about the vessel brought back memories of my childhood holidays in Cleethorpes on the east coast. The sun always seemed to shine and I remember happy hours spent in a wonderland of fairground rides and candy floss. Every year we went for a trip on the Wingfield Castle and I believed my dad when he told me it was named after his granddad who worked so hard as a navvy digging the railway tracks that the company named the ship after him! Whether the story is true or not, I plan to pay a visit to Hartlepool museum where the Wingfield Castle is now on display.

I am wearing a coat and hat made by Mum who used to go to local jumble sales to buy clothes which she unpicked to make into new coats and pinafore dresses for me and my cousins. We were the best-dressed kids in our village thanks to her skill on an old sewing machine.

Maureen Whall, née Winfield, via email

Name that tune

Those three girls kept that poor movie star hanging around for ages, talking in the language that gave us nonnas and pasta. Inspired by a love of Martin Scorcese films, this hit number three in 1984.

A: Robert de Niro's Waiting, Bananarama

Word of the week

Phoney

During the 19th century Fawney men (con artists), practised a ring-dropping scam called the fawney rig. Here they'd conveniently find a gold ring on the street and would offer to sell it to an unsuspecting passer-by for a cut price. The ring, of course, was always a phoney.

Try something new!

Visit your nearest farmers' markets and pick out some fresh produce. See how many different meals you can cook with your goods over a period of one week.

Uncommon knowledge

Honor Blackman left The Avengers and her character Cathy Gale, to join Sean Connery in Goldfinger. There is a nod to this in the show where John Steed mentions he got a Christmas card from Cathy, from Fort Knox.

Recipe of the week

VEGAN SAUSAGE PASTA

SERVES: 4
PREP: 10 mins
COOK: 20 mins

400g (14oz) cherry tomatoes
4 garlic cloves, sliced
3 tbsp olive oil
300g (10.5oz) pack Linda McCartney's Vegetarian Sausages (6)
2 courgettes, trimmed and sliced
Pinch salt
300g (10½oz) pasta tubes
Handful basil leaves

1 Pre-heat the oven to 200°C/ Fan 180°C/ Gas Mark 6. Toss the tomatoes, garlic and 2 tbsp oil in a roasting tin; season. Remove the packaging and film from the sausages but leave in the foil tray. Put the roasting tin and foil tray in the oven for 15 mins, giving each one a toss halfway through.
2 Heat the remaining 1 tbsp oil in a large non-stick frying pan and fry the courgettes with the pinch of salt for about 8 mins, turning regularly until golden. In a separate pan of boiling water, simmer the pasta for 10-12 mins then drain, reserving a cup of pasta water.
3 Remove the courgettes from the frying pan and set aside on a plate. Slice the sausages and add to the pan, frying for a couple of mins, then tip in the pasta, tomatoes, any roasting juices, 2-3 tbsp pasta water and the courgettes. Toss together briefly and serve scattered with basil leaves.

waitrose.com

18 SUNDAY

19 MONDAY

20 TUESDAY

21 WEDNESDAY

22 THURSDAY

23 FRIDAY

24 SATURDAY

Down memory lane

NIGHTS UNDER THE STARS

This holiday snap is of my husband Terry who introduced me to life under canvas. My first taste of camping was in the Scottish Highlands, an experience I shared with hundreds of midges. On our second attempt at a camping holiday I was jerked awake by our ten-year-old daughter screaming: "Mummy, something is eating my hair!". Her long tresses had escaped outside the tent and a large horse was chewing away at them.

It was 45 years before I felt ready to give it another go. As Terry has often remarked: "You don't go camping to sleep." This is so true! Every small sound keeps you awake and then just as you start to drift off – joy of joys – your inflatable mattress starts to deflate. The one advantage of being woken by the dawn chorus is that you manage to cram a lot into your day and still have time for a siesta.

Having progressed to a two-room tent, our priorities are small sites, out of season, with plenty of space between pitches. We are not new age travellers, but old age travellers and have many wonderful memories of nights under the stars.
Niva Poole, Truro

Name that tune

Never a hit for its creator, born Robert Zimmerman, it was Peter, Paul and Mary's cover that got it in the charts. It has since appeared in Forrest Gump and was used in Co-op TV adverts.

A: Blowin' in the Wind, Bob Dylan

Word of the week
Biblioklept
Some words in the English language work hard to sound more impressive than they really are. Biblioklept is a good example. Biblio means book and klept is thought to be derived from the Greek word kleptes which means thief. Put together you simply have someone who steals books.

Try something new!
Set yourself a foodie challenge – go plant based, gluten free or dairy free, or try to cut out sugar for a week!

Uncommon knowledge

Known for Jelly Babies and a particularly long scarf, Tom Baker's Doctor is the fourth and longest reigning incarnation of Doctor Who. His iconic scarf was, however, made by accident. Begonia Pope, the woman responsible for the gargantuan knitting, had unclear instructions, so knitted until she ran out of wool, resulting in the 22ft neck wear.

Recipe of the week

SPICY MEATBALL PASTA BAKE

SERVES: 6
PREP: 5 mins
COOK: 20 mins

1 tbsp olive oil
20 beef meatballs
340g (12oz) jar of tomato and chilli pasta sauce
250g (9oz) frozen grilled vegetable mix
300g (10½ oz) fusilli pasta
50g (2oz) English cheddar cheese, grated

1 Heat the oil in a frying pan and fry the meatballs for 5 mins. Add the sauce to the meatballs with the grilled vegetables and cook, covered, for 5 mins.
2 Meanwhile, cook the pasta in boiling water for 10 mins, drain. Stir into the meatball mixture and transfer to a heatproof serving dish.
3 Sprinkle with cheese and place under a pre-heated grill for 2-3 mins until golden.

Waitose.com

25 SUNDAY

26 MONDAY

27 TUESDAY

28 WEDNESDAY

29 THURSDAY

30 FRIDAY

1 SATURDAY

Down memory lane

LOVE BLOSSOMED

I love the story of how my parents, Charlie and Alice Madeley, met. After my mother lost her fiancé to TB when she was 24 she had no other boyfriends for ten years until she passed a stranger on her way to work.

Having exchanged a polite 'good morning' a few times, Charlie stopped and asked her if she liked flowers. Mum thought he must have been out drinking, but after he introduced himself and convinced her of his sobriety, he promised her flowers.

At lunchtime she was approached by what appeared to be a flower shop on legs. It was Dad with two armsful of gladioli that he had grown on his allotment. He invited her to the cinema to see a Shirley Temple film. It actually turned out to be The Life of a Bengal Tiger, but that didn't seem to matter as they were married on Boxing Day 1938. I was their only child, born in 1944, before Charlie very sadly died of cancer in 1945.

Fortunately, Mum came from a large, loving family so I spent much of my childhood with my delightful nana and granddad, while she went out to work to support us.
Margaret O'Callaghan, Wednesfield

Name that tune

Ladies just want a laugh is the theme of this song that became an Eighties anthem for the singer with giant earrings and bright hair who kickstarted a movement of girl power.

A: Girls Just Want to Have Fun, Cyndi Lauper

Word of the week

Cattywampus

It's hard to say this word without it raising a smile. Its dictionary meaning is 'going bad, awkwardly or in the wrong direction'. While its roots are not clear, some believe the second part may be from the Scottish term wampish, which means to wriggle about.

Try something new!

Go on a wildlife walk. Visit a park, nature reserve or green space. Take a pair of binoculars and see how many species you can identify along the way. Write down their characteristics and use Google to check how many species you identify correctly.

Uncommon knowledge

Clint Eastwood dons his iconic poncho in each of the Dollars Trilogy films. For the filming of the entire trilogy it was never washed, though it was fixed after it was so rudely shot by Ramon.

'There's two kinds of people in this world, those with ponchos and those who dig those with ponchos...'

Recipe of the week

SWEET POTATOES WITH CHICKEN

SERVES: 2
PREP: 5 mins
COOK: 20 mins

2 sweet potatoes
115g (4oz) baby spinach
1 roasted chicken breast fillet, skinned and shredded
1 tsp Dijon mustard
3 tbsp ranch salad dressing
Salt and black pepper

1 Pre-heat the oven to 200°C/Fan 180°C/Gas Mark 6. Prick the potatoes with a fork and microwave on full power for 6 mins, then transfer to the oven on a baking tray for 15 mins.
2 Meanwhile, place the spinach in a large bowl, cover with clingfilm and microwave for 1 min or until just wilted. Squeeze out the excess liquid and roughly chop. Mix together the spinach, chicken, Dijon mustard, salad dressing and season.
3 Cut the potatoes in half and top with the chicken mixture.

Waitrose.com

2 SUNDAY

3 MONDAY

4 TUESDAY

5 WEDNESDAY

6 THURSDAY

7 FRIDAY

8 SATURDAY

Down memory lane

STARGAZING WITH DAD

Here I am with my dad who at different times in his life was a gymnast, an aircraft mechanic and, during the war, a dispatch rider. He was very proud of his family of four daughters and a son and encouraged us all to be educated. He said it was important for girls to have the same opportunities as boys. We could all swim by the age of six and when we were old enough he taught us all to drive on a disused airfield at Stretton.

We spent our holidays in a tiny caravan at Prestatyn. Dad used to take us to visit castles and recount the history of how the English had massacred the Welsh in 1200 AD. At midnight, just as we had settled down in our smelly, army issue sleeping bags, he would order us all out into the field to lie in a circle like the spokes of a wheel. Leaping around like a mad professor in his maroon silk dressing gown, he told us stories about the stars and how pirates knew how to steer their boats guided by the Great Bear, the Seven Sisters and the Pole star. He was truly a unique dad.

Sophia Drew, Prestatyn

Name that tune

All the fun of the fair and a bit of Punch and Judy spirit went into this 1967 oompah classic that saw the girl with the bare feet become a household name.

A: Puppet on a String, Sandie Shaw

Word of the week

**Pneumonoultramicrosco-
-picsilicovolcanoconiosis**
At 45 letters long, P45 (to which it is
sometimes referred), is the longest
English word published in a major
dictionary. This scientific name refers
to a lung disease caused by inhalation
of fine ash and sand dust, however it's
lengthy nature and obscure definitions
means it doesn't get much use!

Try something new!

Listen to a new genre of music - how
about soul, jazz, rock, folk, classical or
Eighties 'alternative'? For inspiration,
find genre-specific playlists via the
Spotify web player at open.spotify.com

Uncommon knowledge

For the first time since the original film,
the plot of The Return of the Pink Panther
(1975) centres around the titular diamond.
The Inspector Clouseau franchise had Peter
Sellers at the helm once more, though the
film did lack David Niven as Phantom.
    The animated TV series spawned
from the title sequence, won an Academy
Award for best Animated Short Film in its
first outing.

Recipe of the week

CHEESE MUFFINS WITH SWEETCORN & SPINACH

MAKES: 12 muffins
PREP: 5 mins
COOK: 20-25 mins

175g (6oz) plain flour
1 tsp bicarbonate of soda
150g (5oz) pre-grated cheese
50g (2oz) baby spinach, shredded
100g (4oz) tinned sweetcorn, drained
2 eggs
150g (5oz) unsalted butter, melted
150ml (5floz) milk

1 Pre-heat the oven to 180°C/Fan 160°C/Gas Mark 4.
2 Combine the flour, bicarbonate, cheese, spinach and sweetcorn in the mixing bowl.
3 Add the eggs, melted butter and milk and mix it all together.
4 Divide the batter evenly into the muffin cases.
5 Bake for 20-25 mins until risen and golden. Serve warm.

Tip: Don't have spinach or sweetcorn? Experiment with your favourite fillings - chopped red pepper, onions or cubed ham make for delicious alternatives. You can also add finely chopped chilli or chilli pepper flakes to add a spicy kick!
Easy Peasy Baking fabflour.co.uk

9 SUNDAY

10 MONDAY

11 TUESDAY

12 WEDNESDAY

13 THURSDAY

14 FRIDAY

15 SATURDAY

Down memory lane

SIMPLY SICK OF SUNDAY SCHOOL

In the Fifties I went to a boarding school near Ashburton in Devon. Every Sunday we were marched off to St John the Baptist church which was about a mile away. Half way through the service the vicar would ask us questions on religious topics and if you got the answers right, you were awarded a stamp.

One day during the service I was suddenly very sick and was promptly rushed outside and told to stay there until I was walked back to school in disgrace. I then had to write a letter of apology and thanks to the lady who had to clear my mess up. After this incident I never again went to Sunday School. Instead I had to learn a passage from the Bible which had to be repeated without fault before I was allowed to sit down to lunch. I must admit I often felt rather smug when I saw everyone else having to set off in bad weather.

All this might sound rather harsh, but Miss Snow who ran the school was a lovely lady and we were all very fond of her.
Jackie Jenkins, Liskeard

Name that tune

Debbie didn't want us to be left listening to the dial tone in this 1978 hit for the peroxide star and her band. The song was later covered by Girls Aloud and Def Leppard.

A: Hanging on the Telephone, Blondie

Word of the week

Clue

Derived from the word clew, which translates to ball of yarn. In Greek mythology Ariadne gave Theseus a ball of yarn to help him find his way out of the Minotaur's labyrinth. Clew later became clue – something that can be 'followed' to solve a mystery!

Try something new!

Enjoy a spa day at home and save the pennies! Simply recreate the atmosphere with a scented candle then give yourself a manicure or pedicure while wearing a soothing face mask.

Uncommon knowledge

The Avengers, a pinnacle of Sixties TV, ran for the majority of the decade. The crime-fighting spy Emma Peel also broke a landmark screen record when, Diana Rigg's character became the first western woman to perform Kung Fu on screen.

Recipe of the week

POACHED EGG & KALE MUFFIN STACKS

SERVES: 1
PREP: 5 mins
COOK: 5 mins

1 courgette, thinly sliced lengthways
1 tbsp olive oil
50g (2oz) kale
2 eggs
1 wholemeal muffin, halved and toasted
1 tbsp soft cheese

1 Brush the courgette slices with a little oil and griddle for 4-5 mins, turning once until softened. Meanwhile, cook the kale in boiling water for 5 mins and drain well.
2 Poach the eggs in a saucepan of boiling water.
3 Spread the muffin with the soft cheese, top with the kale and courgettes then the eggs. Season and serve.

Waitrose.com

16 SUNDAY

17 MONDAY

18 TUESDAY

19 WEDNESDAY

20 THURSDAY

21 FRIDAY

22 SATURDAY

Down memory lane

AND THE WINNER IS...

In 1974 my soldier husband was posted to Northern Ireland for four months while I remained in Catterick Garrison with our young son. To keep myself occupied, I found a job at the Spar supermarket on the camp. I enjoyed the work and must have made a good impression as my boss entered me for the Miss Spar Tyne Tees competition.

On my husband's return we were invited to the Billingham Arms hotel for the Guild of Spar Grocers' annual dinner and dance. I was thrilled when I was chosen to be Miss Spar Tyne Tees 1975 and the picture shows me being presented with my sash. Part of my prize was a three-day shopping and sightseeing trip to London. This included a gala night at the Grosvenor House hotel in Park Lane to choose the national winner of the competition.

I was told later I'd been a close runner-up, but as my boss's son, Michael, won the award for best trainee manager it was felt to be unfair to have two winners from the same shop. But we'd had a fabulous time and it was a great homecoming for my husband after a dangerous tour of duty.
Patricia Rogers, Keighley

Name that tune

You'd get a rush of blood to the head and such a strange feeling following the advice of this 1986 song from the American singer songwriter and former member of The Commodores.

A: Dancing on the Ceiling, Lionel Richie

Word of the week

Dunce

This derogatory term has an unforgiving history. Duns were the so-called followers of philosopher theologian John Duns Scotus, whose work earned him great accolade in the 13th Century. During the Renaissance his teachings were discredited and the term Duns became a way of describing those who followed his outdated ideas.

Try something new!

Take yourself back to your childhood by playing a game you enjoyed, watch an old black and white movie, or perhaps look through an old photo album. You could listen to your favourite artist or band from that time and even recreate your favourite school dinner!

Uncommon knowledge

Young Frankenstein is a parody of all the dark gritty, horror films that came before it. Mel Brooks considered it to be his finest work. The Blind Man's line "I was gonna make espresso" was ad-libbed by Gene Hackman and had to cut straight to black as the entire crew burst out laughing.

Recipe of the week

MINI SHEPHERD'S PIES WITH CRUSHED JERSEY ROYALS

SERVES: 4
PREP: 15 mins
COOK: 45 mins

500g (1.1lb) lamb mince
1 sprig rosemary, finely chopped
1 large onion, diced
2 carrots, diced
1 stick celery, thinly sliced
2 cloves garlic, chopped
400g (14oz) can cherry tomatoes
1 tbsp tomato puree
2 tbsp Worcestershire sauce
500g (1.1lb) Jersey Royal potatoes
40g (1½ oz) butter, melted
10 mint leaves, chopped
Salt and black pepper
Steamed spring cabbage and asparagus to serve

1 Place the lamb mince in a large pan on high heat, for 10 mins to brown. Add the rosemary, onion, carrots, celery and garlic and cook for another 5 mins.
2 Stir in the tomatoes, tomato puree and Worcestershire sauce. Rinse the tomato can with 2 tbsp of water and add to the pan. Bring to the boil and simmer for 15 mins.
3 Meanwhile, boil whole the Jersey Royal potatoes in a large pan, and cook for 10-15 mins until just tender. Drain. Roughly crush using the back of a spoon, stir in the butter, mint and some freshly ground pepper and salt.
4 Preheat the oven to 180°C/Fan 160°C/Gas Mark 4. Divide the lamb mixture between 4 ovenproof dishes or make one large pie if preferred, top with the crushed potatoes and bake for 20-30 mins until golden. Serve with steamed veg alongside.

Jersery Royals

23 SUNDAY

24 MONDAY

25 TUESDAY

26 WEDNESDAY

27 THURSDAY

28 FRIDAY

29 SATURDAY

Down memory lane

IT COULD HAVE BEEN WORSE!

A little while before this photo was taken I had fallen from a big slide in a children's playground in Barking in Essex. It was an accident. I either lost my footing or maybe someone pushed me (we'll never know) but there I was, aged six, flying though the air!

Mum was sitting on a bench with a friend while Dad was strolling close by so they didn't see it happen. A kind gentleman rushed to pick me up and stayed with me until they arrived. We went straight home where I was put to bed. In those days you only called an ambulance as a last resort. However, a doctor was called who said I appeared to be okay despite landing on my cheekbone. He prescribed ice-cream, rest and making me sick in case I had concussion. Mum ignored the last part as she didn't agree!

In a few days I was fine although Mum said the incident had aged her ten years. It hadn't put me off going to the playground, but she made Dad accompany me as she couldn't face it. Eventually, Mum did manage to come and here she is putting on a brave smile.
Linda Kettle, Portsmouth

Name that tune

Recorded since by Barry Manilow, Barbra Streisand and Michael Crawford, it was initially a West End actress turned Radio 2 presenter who made a hit of this instantly memorable song about a once-glamorous moggy.

A: Memory, Elaine Paige

Word of the week

Kerfuffle

Still in use today in Britain, Kerfuffle has had numerous different spellings including curfuffle, carfuffle and even gefuffle. Derived from the old Scots verb fuffle, which means to disorder or confuse, the ker part is thought to be from the Scots Gaelic 'car' which means to twist something around. Together you have a fuss or commotion over nothing.

Try something new!

Learn the basics of a new craft, from needlework and embroidery, to macrame and applique. For something a little simpler, there are lots of easy-to-follow ideas to be found online on Pinterest.

Uncommon knowledge

Bonnie and Clyde, starring Faye Dunaway and Warren Beatty, was hated by Jack Warner, after seeing an advance screening. Warner Bros had such little faith that they offered Beatty 40 per cent gross instead of a fee. The film went on to make more than 50 million dollars...

Recipe of the week

ROSEMARY CHICKEN TRAY BAKE

SERVES: 2
PREP: 15 mins
COOK: 30 mins

2 x 150g skinned boneless chicken breasts
4 spring onions, trimmed and halved
100g (4oz) pumpkin, peeled, deseeded and cubed
2 courgettes, sliced
6 cherry tomatoes, halved
a few sprigs of rosemary
4 unpeeled garlic cloves
Spray oil
Salt and freshly ground black pepper
Balsamic vinegar for drizzling

1 Pre-heat the oven to 200°C/Fan 180°C/Gas Mark 6.
2 Make 2–3 slashes in the top of each chicken breast with a sharp knife. Place in a roasting pan with the spring onions, pumpkin, courgettes and tomatoes. Tuck the rosemary and garlic into the gaps between the vegetables and spray lightly with oil. Season with salt and pepper.
3 Roast in the oven for 30 mins, or until the chicken is cooked right through and golden brown and the vegetables are tender.
4 Squeeze the garlic cloves out of their skins and stir into the vegetables. Serve garnished with fresh rosemary and drizzled with balsamic vinegar.
one2onediet.com

30 SUNDAY

31 MONDAY

1 TUESDAY

2 WEDNESDAY

3 THURSDAY

4 FRIDAY

5 SATURDAY

Down memory lane

FROM CARAVAN TO COUNCIL HOUSE

When we married in 1957 rented accommodation was in short supply so we moved in with my sister-in-law and her husband. After our first baby was born we needed more room and moved into the caravan in the photo. It was lovely to have our own space.

By then we were expecting our second baby who was born six weeks early after I had locked myself out and fell, trying to climb in the window. She was delivered on Kingston Bridge by the paramedic.

The caravan site was a very friendly one and we were never short of a babysitter, but my mother was appalled that we had to get water from a standpipe and dig our own soakaway for the toilet. My husband had an old motorbike with a sidecar in which he used to take us to his sister's for a bath every week.

My mother harassed the council on our behalf and luckily before the unusually cold winter of 1964 we were offered a council house. It was very old, had one cold tap in the kitchen and an outside toilet, but what luxury!

Ann Evans, Portchester

Name that tune

Written to mark the birth of this performer's daughter, this opens with the cries of a newborn and features a classic harmonica solo. It was performed for the Diamond Jubilee Concert to describe the Queen.

A: Isn't She Lovely, Stevie Wonder

Word of the week
Nightmare
Surprisingly the 'mare' part of nightmare has nothing to do with horses. Instead, it's a name for a female evil spirit who would suffocate its victims while they slept. Now that truly is the stuff of nightmares!

Try something new!
Why not upcycle a piece of furniture? Revive an old chair with a sand and paint or recover a side table with self-adhesive film. Scour the charity shops and attach vintage knobs to a chest of drawers!

Uncommon knowledge

With a salary of $750,000, Audrey Hepburn became the second highest-paid actress, behind Elizabeth Taylor. It wasn't all sunshine for her on the set of Breakfast at Tiffany's however. She once commented that throwing the cat out on the street was the most distasteful moment of her career, and, she hated danish pastries. The iconic opening scene must've been quite the culinary challenge.

Recipe of the week

VEGGIE BAKED EGGS

SERVES: 2
PREP: 5 mins
COOK: 15 mins

80g (3oz) mushrooms
1 tbsp of olive oil or coconut oil
80g (3oz) spinach, washed
150g (5oz) chopped tomatoes
4 British Lion eggs
1 tsp chilli flakes
1 tbsp Parmesan, freshly grated
1 tsp lightly toasted pine nuts, chopped

1 Pre-heat the oven to 200°C/Fan 180°C/Gas Mark 6.
2 Fry the mushrooms in the olive oil until caramelised.
3 Heat a small saucepan and add the spinach. If you have just washed the spinach then there is no need to add any water to the pan - there will be enough moisture on the leaves.
4 Divide the cooked spinach between two dishes or four small ramekins. Add the cooked mushrooms. Put a generous spoon of chopped tomato into each dish.
5 Make wells in the dishes and crack in the eggs into each dish, either two for a larger dish or one in each using four smaller dishes. Sprinkle over a pinch of chilli flakes, the grated Parmesan and the pine nuts. Bake for 15 mins in the oven or until the eggs are just cooked.

Eggs British Lion Eggs eggrecipes.co.uk

6 SUNDAY

7 MONDAY

8 TUESDAY

9 WEDNESDAY

10 THURSDAY

11 FRIDAY

12 SATURDAY

Down memory lane

LOVE ON THE NILE

My husband Laurie and I met during the war when we were both on a boat trip on the river Nile. He was an airman and I was a WAAF stationed in Egypt. We were courting for six months before he was posted back to the UK. A few months later my own posting came through and on my second day home we were able to meet in Bangor near where he was based. It was a wonderful day. Realising we wanted our future to be together we became engaged and married a year later.

I had joined the WAAFs on the persuasion of my mother who said she had always wanted to travel and as it happened I was in the first contingent to be sent abroad. We were issued with khaki uniforms and pith helmets, but not told our destination. After a few weeks at sea we docked at Port Said from where we were transported to our quarters on the banks of the Nile. We were made very welcome and there were never any wallflowers at camp dances! I was also the soloist at station concerts singing popular numbers such as As Time Goes By.
Beryl Corry, St Ives

Name that tune

Now the name of a musical and a 1973 movie, this was the first hit for an iconic rock 'n' roll singer with trademark glasses who said 'goodbye' all too soon.

A: That'll Be The Day, Buddy Holly

Word of the week

Throttlebottom

Some words just can't help but make you chuckle and throttlebottom is one of them. Named after Alexander Throttlebottom, a character in the musical comedy Of Thee I Sing, throttlebottom means an innocuously inept and futile person in public office.

Try something new!

Buy a new or unusual food at the supermarket. Visit the world foods aisle and put the first thing that catches your eye into your basket or trolley!

Uncommon knowledge

One of the only films made by Marilyn Monroe Productions, The Prince and the Showgirl, despite its pedigree, was not a box office hit. Even Laurence Olivier directing, and Monroe, fresh out of training with Lee Strasberg could not save the flick. It did serve its purpose though, after proving she could make it on her own 20th Century Fox awarded her a much bigger contract.

Recipe of the week

GINGER BREAD & BUTTER PUDDING

SERVES: 6
PREP: 10 mins
COOK: 40 mins

6 thin slices of day-old buttered white bread (crusts removed)
25g (1oz) caster sugar
50g (2oz) Opies Stem Ginger in Syrup, finely chopped, plus additional 2 tsps of syrup from the jar
Handful of dried fruit (optional)
2 eggs
600ml (20 floz) milk

1 Cut each slice of buttered bread into small triangles and place half into a 1 litre buttered oven dish.
2 Sprinkle with half the sugar and add the finely chopped ginger plus optional dried fruit. Top with the remaining bread, butter side up. Sprinkle with the remaining sugar and ginger.
3 Beat the eggs, milk and ginger syrup together and strain into oven dish, over the bread.
4 Allow to stand for 30 mins then bake in a pre-heated oven at 160°C/ Fan 140°C/Gas 3 for 45 mins or until set and golden on top.

opiesfoods.com

13 SUNDAY

14 MONDAY

15 TUESDAY

16 WEDNESDAY

17 THURSDAY

18 FRIDAY

19 SATURDAY

Down memory lane

MY KIND AND GENTLE DAD

For many years my dad was a gardener for the Duke of Connaught at Bagshot Park in Surrey. We lived in a Victorian cottage in the park which was bequeathed to him on the death of the duke.

Born in 1909, Dad was a kind and gentle man who loved his work. He had been taught copperplate handwriting at school and was excellent at English and maths. He knew the Latin names of all the plants. When he took my brother and myself for walks in the woods he could name every tree and wildflower. He taught us which fungi were edible and which ones were poisonous.

When I was six he gave me a small patch of my own in the corner of the garden. I loved being outside, digging the earth and watching things grow. As a small child, my brother was never far from Dad's side. Holding on to the handle of the huge mower as Dad navigated it up and down, his little legs moved like pistons to keep up. Dad made us a swing at the top of our large garden. We swung so high we could see over the tall fence to the cornfield beyond.
Sylvia Washington via email

Name that tune

Reflecting on how friends can be just as important as family, this song's creator regularly performed it alongside James Taylor. It shares its name with a song in the Toy Story movie.

A: You've Got a Friend, Carole King

Word of the week

Waggish

Meaning funny in a clever way, this merry word sounds as though it could have been inspired by man's best friend. However, its history is far more bleak as it's likely derived from the word waghalter – a person who was destined to be hung.

Try something new!

Go on a spontaneous weekend break. If you're feeling daring, find a map of the UK and point to a destination whilst wearing a blindfold. Should your finger points to nowhere in particular, visit the nearest town or city to that location.

Uncommon knowledge

"I'm a simple woman with simple tastes, and I want to be wooed".
"Ooh, you can be as 'wude' as you like with me"...

Carry on Matron ties with Carry On Abroad as having the most series regulars at a total of 11, with only Jim Dale and Peter Butterworth missing. Jack Douglas would make his series debut with a small cameo in this film, and the film's producer and director were both so impressed that they sent him a crate of Dom Pérignon as thanks.

Recipe of the week

POTATOES WITH PEPPERS & CHORIZO

SERVES: 6
PREP: 10 mins
COOK: 45 mins

100ml (3½floz) olive oil
5 garlic cloves, thinly sliced
2 onions, finely chopped
2 red peppers, seeded and finely chopped
3 tomatoes, roughly chopped
300g (10oz) semi-cured chorizo, cut into 2cm slices
½ tbsp hot pimentón (or use sweet pimentón and 1 dried cayenne chilli)
1 kg (2lb 3oz) floury potatoes, peeled and cut into chunks
2 tbsp red wine or sherry vinegar
2 sprigs of fresh thyme, leaves picked (optional)
Salt and freshly ground black pepper
Bread, to serve

1 Heat the olive oil in a large pan over a medium heat and add the garlic, onion and red pepper. Fry until golden, about 15 mins.
2 Add the chopped tomatoes, chorizo, pimentón, potato chunks and cook for a further 5 mins.
3 Add the vinegar, thyme leaves (if using) and 1.5 litres of water. Season and bring to the boil. Simmer for about 25 mins until the potatoes are cooked.
4 Serve immediately with some good bread.

The Tapas Revolution by Omar Allibhoy, available on Ebury Digital

20 SUNDAY

21 MONDAY

22 TUESDAY

23 WEDNESDAY

24 THURSDAY

25 FRIDAY

26 SATURDAY

Down memory lane

THE BEAUTIFUL GAME

My dad, Jimmy 'Mac', lived, talked and breathed football. He played for clubs all around Lancashire and even, at one time, for Pwllheli FC. The week before he and Mum were to be married an unexpected draw for Dad's team resulted in a replay scheduled for – you've guessed it – his wedding day! After heated family discussions, the service was switched to the morning and Dad played in the afternoon, when this photo of the newly-weds was taken.

As soon as my brother and I were old enough to withstand the wind and the rain, we were taken to matches to cheer him on. Holidays were torture for Dad because he had to phone home to hear his team's results. We'd sit in the hotel or caravan, hoping hard that they had won.

Of course Dad was a big fan of Match of the Day. If the result of the game was shown earlier we had to dive in front of the TV screen, cover Dad's eyes, shout or turn the sound down quickly. Football was as much part of my Dad as him kissing me goodnight and telling me stupid jokes. I miss him every day.
Julie McKiernan via email

Name that tune

Initially considered too 'weird' for radio, this mock opera song, referencing astronomers and Italian clowns, owes much of its success to Kenny Everett. It is the only record to have been a Christmas No 1 twice.

A: Bohemian Rhapsody, Queen

Word of the week

Bumfuzzle

This delightfully silly word means to confuse or to fluster. Likely to be a derived from a combination of bamboozle (to deceive) and fuzzle (to confuse), this amazing word has been in use (albeit not widely) since the 19th Century.

Try something new!

Write a mood journal. Check in with yourself morning, afternoon and evening to see how you're feeling, specifically taking note of how you feel emotionally and physically. If you can't think of the words, try to illustrate your feelings using drawings or doodles instead.

Uncommon knowledge

It's time we reverse the polarity of the neutron flow! Jon Pertwee took over the reins as the third Doctor in Doctor Who, but he was the first to do so in colour. For much of his tenure, due to BBC budgeting restraints, they lacked the money to fling the Doctor to far-off planets, so they had his wings clipped by the Time Lords, who forced his regeneration and broke his TARDIS, stranding him on the much cheaper Earth.

Recipe of the week

CHOCOLATE PUDDING

SERVES: 6
PREP: 10 mins
COOK: 25 mins

50g (2oz) butter
75g (3oz) caster sugar
4 large British Lion eggs, separated
300ml (½pt) milk
50g (2oz) self-raising flour
4tbsp cocoa

1 Pre-heat the oven to 180°C/Fan 160°C/ Gas Mark 4.
2 Lightly oil 6 x 175ml (6floz) ovenproof dishes. In a large bowl, cream the butter and sugar together using an electric whisk until the mixture is pale and fluffy.
3 Add the egg yolks and beat again until smooth. Add the milk, flour and cocoa and blend again using the electric whisk until smooth and quite runny.
4 Wash the whisk heads, then in a clean bowl, whisk the egg whites until they form soft peaks. Gently fold into the chocolate mixture. Divide between the prepared dishes. Bake for 12 mins or until risen. Carefully transfer to serving plates and serve straight away.

British Lion Eggs eggrecipes.co.uk

27 SUNDAY

28 MONDAY

29 TUESDAY

30 WEDNESDAY

1 THURSDAY

2 FRIDAY

3 SATURDAY

Down memory lane

IN PERFECT HARMONY

Despite being born into a family with no musical affinity, my granddad Ernest was naturally gifted and had perfect pitch. He taught himself to play the piano and the organ and played in various bands before becoming a cinema organist in the era of silent films.

In 1923 he married Kathleen, a violinist he had met while playing at the cinema in Ramsgate. Later that year he left for Australia to perform in the new theatres and cinemas being opened by the Hoyts company. He took an apartment in the Elizabeth Bay area of Sydney where Kathleen and their baby son joined him. From there they moved to Melbourne where my father was born in 1928. Ernest's orchestra was a great success and frequently broadcast dance music on local radio.

The advent of talking pictures coupled with the economic depression resulted in a downturn in demand and the couple decided to return to England. They settled back in Ramsgate where Kathleen played in a hotel's Palm Court orchestra. Ernest had his own orchestra through the summer season and in the winter months he toured the country selling pianos.
Elizabeth Lowe via email

Name that tune

The Four Seasons frontman lent his unique falsetto voice to this theme tune to one of the biggest movies of the Seventies that certainly had plenty of groove and meaning.

A: Grease is the Word, Frankie Valli!

Word of the week

Sneeze

Some scholars believe that sneeze beginning with an 's' was a case of mistaken identity. Thought to be derived from the Old English word fneosan, it became fnese in Middle English but the 'f' was mistaken for an 's', bringing us snese. Of course, nowadays we spell it as sneeze.

Try something new!

Plant bulbs in a window box. They'll need at least two inches of soil over their tops, but three to four inches is best – so make sure that the window box is deep enough to provide the space necessary. Water frequently as the stems grow and start to bloom, ensuring the soil never dries out.

Uncommon knowledge

It's only a day away, or rather two years if you were one of the many hopeful Annies trying for the titular role, the casting of which took 8,000 interviews before landing on Aileen Quinn. Famous hopefuls included Drew Barrymore for the lead, Jack Nicholson for Daddy Warbucks, and Mick Jagger for Rooster.

Recipe of the week

BEEF AND ALE PIE

SERVES: 4
PREP: 10 mins
COOK: 2 hours

900g (16oz) stewing beef, diced
25g (1oz) flour, seasoned with salt and pepper, plus extra for dusting
100g (4oz) butter
2 cloves garlic, roughly chopped
2 medium carrots, roughly chopped
150g (5oz) mushrooms, sliced
2 sprigs fresh thyme
1 bay leaf
100g (4oz) Opies Cocktail Onions
100g (4oz) Opies Pickled Walnuts, sliced
400ml (14floz) good quality ale
500ml (17½floz) beef stock
2 free-range egg yolks, beaten
300g (10oz) ready-made rolled puff pastry

1 Roll meat in the seasoned flour to cover fully. Heat half the butter in a saucepan and add the meat. Sear all over until golden brown.
2 Add the veg, herbs, cocktail onions and walnuts, then pour in the ale and stock. Bring to a simmer, then cover with a lid and gently simmer on the stove for 1½ hours.
3 Preheat the oven to 220°C/Fan 200°C/Gas Mark 7.
4 Once cooked, stir through the remaining butter and tip into an ovenproof serving dish.
5 Brush the edge of the dish with the beaten egg. Unroll the pastry and place over the dish. Pinch the edges of the dish so that the pastry will stick to it and trim off any pastry from around the edge. Cut the leftover pastry into leaves and brush the underside with beaten egg and stick to the pastry.
6 Brush the top of the pie with the remaining beaten egg and bake in the oven for 20-30 mins until the pastry is golden brown on top.

opiesfoods.com

4 SUNDAY

_____

5 MONDAY

_____

6 TUESDAY

_____

7 WEDNESDAY

_____

8 THURSDAY

_____

9 FRIDAY

_____

10 SATURDAY

_____

Down memory lane

CHRISTMAS IN GERMANY

As my father served in the Guards for 27 years, our family lived in many different places. This photo of my sister Hazel (on the right) perched on a neighbour's horse was taken when we were based in Dusseldorf in Germany.

We lived in a beautiful three-storey house and had a maid and a gardener. The garden had numerous fruit trees as well as blackcurrants, redcurrants and strawberries in abundance. I vividly recall going with our maid to a Christmas market in Cologne where a bear was standing on its hind legs at the entrance. On Christmas Eve we followed the German tradition of placing a piece of coal under our pillow to ensure St Nicholas visited us during the night.

From Germany we went to Ireland where my brother Reg was born. In Coronation year we had a party with trestle tables all along the street. The following year we returned to England. Although my schooling was disrupted by so many moves, I managed to get six GCE 'O' levels and feel my life was enhanced by living in other countries.

Barbara Lines, Worthing

Name that tune

The weather forecasters can usually talk of nothing else at this time of year – all the fault of King of the crooners whose song is also a 1954 movie of the same name.

A: White Christmas, Bing Crosby

Word of the week

Quiz

Legend has it that a Dublin theatre owner made a bet that he could introduce a new word into the English language in just 24 hours. Overnight he had the word 'quiz' painted on walls throughout the city. By the following morning everyone knew it well and he won his bet.

Try something new!

Watch the sunrise... there's something magical about watching the beginning of a new day. For a colourful sky, check the weather forecast – look for a day with a ridge of high pressure and light winds. Then check what time the sun is expected to rise where you live and set your alarm clock.

Uncommon knowledge

Saint, Persuader, and 00 Agent. Introduced to the organisation by Audrey Hepburn, Sir Roger Moore served as a Unicef Ambassador, helping to raise over $90 million to combat iodine deficiency across the world. Knighted for his humanitarian work, Moore was also given the Order of Arts and Letters by the French government. Forever modest, Moore attributed his successful career to "99 per cent luck".

Recipe of the week

CAMEMBERT & CRANBERRY TARTS

SERVES: 12
PREP: 10 mins
COOK: 30 mins

200g (7oz) plain flour
100g (4oz) salted butter, cold and cubed
1 tbsp cold water
1 wheel of Camembert cheese, around 250g (9oz)
1 jar of cranberry sauce

1 Pre-heat the oven to 200°C/Fan 180°C/Gas Mark 4. In the large mixing bowl, bring together the flour and cold, cubed butter to form a crumb consistency. Add in the cold water and work to form a dough.
2 Roll the dough out to a 5mm thickness on a lightly floured surface and cut out rounds, pressing each one into the muffin tray to form the tart shells. You will need to bring the dough offcuts together and re-roll to make 12.
3 Prick each tart case base with a fork to stop them rising and place in the oven for 15 mins to blind bake.
4 Remove the rind from the cheese and divide into 12 equal portions. Place a portion into each tart case and return to the oven for a further 15 mins.
5 Allow to cool slightly before placing tarts on a serving platter and topping each one with ½ tbsp of cranberry sauce.

Easy Peasy Baking fabflour.co.uk

11 SUNDAY

12 MONDAY

13 TUESDAY

14 WEDNESDAY

15 THURSDAY

16 FRIDAY

17 SATURDAY

Down memory lane

THE SEASON FOR CHARITY

I will never forget Christmas 2002. My husband and I were visiting our son who was working with a charity called Hands of Mercy International near Manila in the Philippines. Friends of his invited us to visit the island of Cebu to help supply a Christmas meal to people who were living in poverty.

A school had given permission for the event to be held in its grounds and the local church organised buses to transport the families. It was amazing to see hundreds of men, women and children arriving and there was a great air of excitement. The children were particularly fascinated to see two elderly white people and they loved having their photos taken. One little girl told me: "You look so beautiful!". In fact, I was feeling hot and sticky and far from beautiful with the sun beating down.

The cooks had worked for hours to make this a special occasion. My husband and I took plates of food round to the families who were sitting in groups on the grass. Seeing their delight made me feel very humble and brought tears to my eyes.

Frances Gunn, Luton

Name that tune

Strap in and buckle up for this ever-popular festive tune, originally recorded in 1986 although written many years earlier when the performer was sat in his wife's Austin Mini driving to Middlesbrough.

A: Driving Home for Christmas, Chris Rea

Word of the week

Lackadaisical

Listless, lethargic, lazy and without interest, all conjure up a picture of someone who is lackadaisical. It's thought to originate from an old medieval saying 'alack-a-day', which would be used to express dismay or regret.

Try something new!

Fly a kite. Find a wide-open space on a breezy day. Unwind the string about four metres and ask a friend or family member to take the kite away from you while you hold tight on the string. Get them to launch it upwards into the wind and pull the string tight to make the kite climb higher.

Uncommon knowledge

The rights for Casino Royale remained contested until the version starring Daniel Craig in 2006. Until then, the 1967 spy parody with David Niven would be the only time fans would get a chance to see the likes of Vesper Lynd, in this film played by Ursula Andress (formerly Honey Ryder in Dr No). Depending on your preference, the ill-fated 1967 Casino Royale can be forgiven or condemned further for giving us Dusty Springfield's The Look of Love.

Recipe of the week

CHRISTMAS PARTY REINDEER CAKES

SERVES: 12
PREP: 10 mins
COOK: 20 mins

260g (9oz) butter
110g (4oz)caster sugar
2 large eggs
110g (4oz) self-raising flour
300g (10oz) icing sugar
3 tbsp cocoa powder
Edible eyes (available at major supermarkets)
24 pretzels
12 Christmas cupcake cases
2 packs (16g) Fruit Bowl Strawberry Peelers

1 Pre-heat your oven to 180°C/Fan 160°C/Gas Mark 4.
2 Beat 110g (4oz) of the butter and all of the caster sugar together until fluffy.
3 Whisk in the eggs. Add the flour until combined
4 Spoon the mixture evenly into the cupcakes cases.
5 Bake for 15 mins or until a skewer placed in the centre of each cake comes out clean. Leave on a wire rack to cool.
6 Meanwhile, make the butter cream. Whisk the remaining butter until soft, add the icing sugar and cocoa powder and mix until smooth.
7 Once the cakes are cool, pipe the butter cream on top using a thick nozzle.
8 Chop each Fruit Bowl Strawberry Peeler into six so you have 12 pieces. Push one of the Peeler pieces into the centre of the butter cream on each cake
9 Take two pretzels and place on the top of the cupcake to make antlers.
10 Place two of the edible eyes between the antlers and the Peelers to create your Christmas reindeer!
Fruit Bowl fruit-bowl.com

18 SUNDAY

19 MONDAY

20 TUESDAY

21 WEDNESDAY

22 THURSDAY

23 FRIDAY

24 SATURDAY

Down memory lane

MY BEST CHRISTMAS EVER

The Christmas that stands out in my memory is 1956 when I was aged nine. Near my home was a toyshop called Scott's and displayed in the window was the most beautiful walkie talkie doll. She was top of my wish list and every day on my way home from school I would stop to talk to her. I gave her a name, Janet, because she was very real to me.

Then one day to my utter dismay she was no longer there. You will of course guess what had happened, but I was heartbroken and thought that I would never see her again. On Christmas morning I was overjoyed to find her peeping out of my Santa sack. I'm told that I was not a bit interested in opening any of my other gifts as I only wanted to play with the doll of my dreams.

Janet had a long life and although her body deteriorated, her head and blonde wig remained her crowning glory. Eventually she went the way of many dolls of a certain age, but I will never forget her and that truly wonderful Christmas.

Lynette Jones, Winterbourne

Name that tune

Bad weather and the start of the week just did nothing to raise the spirits of these special singing siblings. It was kept from number one only by Carole King's I Feel The Earth Move.

A: Rainy Days and Mondays, The Carpenters

Word of the week

Rumball

Rumball Night was the old 18th Century name for Christmas Eve. Back then it was on Rumball Night that you'd enjoy a delicious rumball feast - instead of Christmas Day. Rum ball is also the name for the truffle-like sweets flavoured with chocolate and rum that are often served at Christmas.

Try something new!

Go cloud watching. On a warm day, find a patch of grass - from your garden, a park or a hill - and lie back and watch the clouds go by. With a little imagination, see how many shapes you can see in the clouds.

Uncommon knowledge

Mary Poppins was a labour of love for Walt Disney, mostly because of the difficulty he had had in securing the rights. Though PL Travers hated the film, Disney loved it. In particular Feed the Birds, which very quickly became his favourite song, often popping by the Sherman Bros studio to request a personal performance.

Recipe of the week

POSH SCRAMBLED EGGS & SMOKED SALMON CROISSANTS

SERVES: 4
PREP: 5 mins
COOK: 5 mins

1 pack of St Pierre All Butter Croissants (four-pack)
6 eggs
50ml (2 floz) milk
Large knob of butter
100g (4oz) smoked salmon
Fresh chives, chopped
4 tsps cream cheese
Black pepper

1 Warm the croissants as per the instructions on the pack.
2 Meanwhile, make the scrambled egg by whisking the eggs with milk and season with pepper.
3 Heat the eggs through in a non-stick pan on a low heat with lots of butter, stir occasionally until gently but not overcooked and stir in the chopped fresh chives at the end.
4 Slice the warm croissants in half, then spread cream cheese on the bottom half. Add the fluffy scrambled egg and a layer of smoked salmon and finish with a few more chives before placing the top of the croissant back on.
5 Serve with your celebratory drink of choice!
stpierregroupe.com

25 SUNDAY

26 MONDAY

27 TUESDAY

28 WEDNESDAY

29 THURSDAY

30 FRIDAY

31 SATURDAY

Down memory lane

WINTER IN OUR FIRST HOME

This is me with my daughter in the caravan that my husband and I bought for £600 when we were married in 1962. We were lucky enough to be on a small site with only five other caravans so we had a fenced-in grassed area at the front and a vegetable patch at the back. We also had a shed and a lean-to that housed my gran's old mangle. I did my washing outside which was fine in the summer, but cold in the winter.

Our first winter was a bad one. We woke to find snow on our bed (it had come through the vents). The water bucket and communal sink were frozen solid so we had to fetch water from the site owner's house. Gran's mangle cracked in the cold!

In 1966 my son was born in the caravan with only the local midwife in attendance. It was cosy and I used to love lying in bed listening to the rain outside. I have good memories of our four years there, but I was very glad of the extra space when we moved in to the bungalow my husband and his brother built for us.

Jan Fower, Salisbury

Name that tune

Written by a Motown husband and wife, there was no limit to the success this song could reach so that nothing could keep it from propelling its singer to 'supreme' new heights.

A: Ain't No Mountain High Enough,
Diana Ross

Word of the week

Yulestarn

Yule is thought to be linked to the Old Norse word jól and can be traced as far back as the 8th Century. Yulestarn, a Scottish dialect word, is a continuation of this and is the name given to the brightest star that can be seen on Christmas night.

Try something new!

Do a car boot sale. It's a great way to declutter your home, make extra space or generate extra cash to buy something new or do something new. Contact your local council to find the ones nearest to you.

Uncommon knowledge

From the mind who brought you James Bond, comes a fun family film about a down-on-his-luck inventor. Ian Fleming's eight-year-old son, whom he had nicknamed 003-and-a-half, complained to him that he never made stories for him, and so came Chitty Chitty Bang Bang.

In a bid to capitalise on the success of Mary Poppins, Albert Broccoli produced the film and hired Dick Van Dyke as the lead and the Sherman Bros for the music.

Recipe of the week

THE PERFECT CHRISTMAS ROAST POTATOES

SERVES: 6
PREP: 10 mins
COOK: 65 mins

2 tbsp oil (sunflower, vegetable, rapeseed) or 30g (1oz) fat (duck or goose fat)
700g (1½ lb) King Edwards, peeled and quartered

1 Pre-heat the oven to 200°C/Fan 180°C/Gas Mark 6.
2 Put the oil or fat into a large roasting tin and place in the oven for 10 mins.
3 Add the potatoes to cold water and bring to the boil. Do not leave the potatoes in the water for more than 10 mins in total.
4 Drain the potatoes well and shake the pan to rough up the edges. Carefully pour the hot oil or fat into the pan of potatoes making sure they are well coated. Tip the potatoes into the roasting tin, spreading them out evenly.
5 Roast in the oven for approximately 45 mins, turning twice. Serve immediately.

provenance-potatoes.co.uk

2022 year-to-view calendar

JANUARY

M		3	10	17	24	31
Tu		4	11	18	25	
W		5	12	19	26	
Th		6	13	20	27	
F		7	14	21	28	
Sa	1	8	15	22	29	
Su	2	9	16	23	30	

FEBRUARY

M		7	14	21	28	
Tu	1	8	15	22		
W	2	9	16	23		
Th	3	10	17	24		
F	4	11	18	25		
Sa	5	12	19	26		
Su	6	13	20	27		

MARCH

M		7	14	21	28	
Tu	1	8	15	22	29	
W	2	9	16	23	30	
Th	3	10	17	24	31	
F	4	11	18	25		
Sa	5	12	19	26		
Su	6	13	20	27		

APRIL

M		4	11	18	25	
Tu		5	12	19	26	
W		6	13	20	27	
Th		7	14	21	28	
F	1	8	15	22	29	
Sa	2	9	16	23	30	
Su	3	10	17	24		

MAY

M		2	9	16	23	30
Tu		3	10	17	24	31
W		4	11	18	25	
Th		5	12	19	26	
F		6	13	20	27	
Sa		7	14	21	28	
Su	1	8	15	22	29	

JUNE

M		6	13	20	27	
Tu		7	14	21	28	
W	1	8	15	22	29	
Th	2	9	16	23	30	
F	3	10	17	24		
Sa	4	11	18	25		
Su	5	12	19	26		

JULY

M		4	11	18	25	
Tu		5	12	19	26	
W		6	13	20	27	
Th		7	14	21	28	
F	1	8	15	22	29	
Sa	2	9	16	23	30	
Su	3	10	17	24	31	

AUGUST

M	1	8	15	22	29	
Tu	2	9	16	23	30	
W	3	10	17	24	31	
Th	4	11	18	25		
F	5	12	19	26		
Sa	6	13	20	27		
Su	7	14	21	28		

SEPTEMBER

M		5	12	19	26	
Tu		6	13	20	27	
W		7	14	21	28	
Th	1	8	15	22	29	
F	2	9	16	23	30	
Sa	3	10	17	24		
Su	4	11	18	25		

OCTOBER

M		3	10	17	24	31
Tu		4	11	18	25	
W		5	12	19	26	
Th		6	13	20	27	
F		7	14	21	28	
Sa	1	8	15	22	29	
Su	2	9	16	23	30	

NOVEMBER

M		7	14	21	28	
Tu	1	8	15	22	29	
W	2	9	16	23	30	
Th	3	10	17	24		
F	4	11	18	25		
Sa	5	12	19	26		
Su	6	13	20	27		

DECEMBER

M		5	12	19	26	
Tu		6	13	20	27	
W		7	14	21	28	
Th	1	8	15	22	29	
F	2	9	16	23	30	
Sa	3	10	17	24	31	
Su	4	11	18	25		

RELAX & UNWIND

Jolly, jolly sixpence!

*Writer Marion Clarke and **Yours** readers recall how we earnt – and spent – our pocket money*

Whether you were a spendthrift who blew it all at the sweet shop, or a canny saver who put some by for a rainy day, pocket money had to be earned – usually by doing household chores.

Every penny I earned by (reluctantly!) doing the washing-up went towards the magic sum of seven and sixpence needed to buy the latest Enid Blyton book. If only I'd kept those first editions – they are worth a whole lot more now!

To earn her sixpence a week **Rosemary Medland** had to fetch the eggs from the chicken run, put the dried crockery away and put clean pillowcases on the pillows. "Sometimes I spent it on crayons or sweets but mostly I spent it on a saving stamp to put in a book. When it was full I got eight pounds to take

on my seaside holiday."

In pre-decimal days, sixpence was pretty much the going rate for pocket money and **Audrey Court** remembers precisely where each precious penny went. "Twopence had to go into a Post Office savings account. Twopence to Mother who saved it for me to buy presents for my aunts and grandmother at Christmas and twopence for me to spend. A trip to Woolworths to buy sweets was a weekly highlight."

Compared with Rosemary and Audrey, **Joyce Dunscombe** was a high earner – she was paid a whole shilling for running errands for her Auntie Mary on a Saturday morning. "When I was a bit older, I babysat for a neighbour and got half-a-crown which went a long way in those days."

Although money did indeed go a long way back then, **Joyce Dickins** and her sister practised a little 'creative accounting' to make it go further... "We were given one penny for the Sunday School collection, but

never told Mother that we spent half of that on sweets." (Joyce scraped together an extra penny by washing doorsteps for people on Saturdays.)

Audrey Warwick's parents were more alert than Joyce's mum to the possibility of cheating. "We were given tenpence to go to the local cinema and instructed not to sit in the sixpenny seats (which were too near the screen) in order to spend the fourpence change on sweets."

In the Sixties, **Rose Janes** had a shilling from her mum

Blast From The Past

and sixpence from her dad each week. "I'm not sure why they gave me money separately. I earned extra by picking blackberries, mushrooms, mistletoe and holly which my mother used to sell on my behalf."

A more traditional way for youngsters to earn some extra money was a paper round. **Thomas Beales'** father made him a handcart from an old pram to carry his load of newspapers. "I would peddle my trade around the streets, calling 'Star, News and Standard!' and my regular customers would flock out of their homes to buy a paper, usually telling me to keep the change."

Hazel Anderson didn't keep her earnings, instead she contributed them to the housekeeping. "In 1948 when I was 12, I had three paper rounds – morning, evening and Sunday. I received 12s 6d, all of which I gave to my mum to help with the family finances."

When **Ivy Lewis** had her first job at the age of 14 she handed her weekly pay packet of 15 shillings to her mother every Friday. "She gave me half-a-crown pocket money out of which I had to buy my own snacks and put some money in the collection plate in church on Sunday. Being the big sister, I gave my two younger brothers and sister a penny each pocket money. They would run straight out to buy a stick of liquorice!"

Friday was also the day when **Daphne Kitchen's** uncle Cyril used to give her twopence on his way home from work. "The choice of how to spend those two pennies was no problem. In summertime, a 'specky' orange (Mrs Jameson at the fruit and veg shop would cut the specky bits out with a knife). In the winter, a drawing book and a packet of crayons to use by the fire.

I wonder how today's children, who apparently receive £7 pocket money, would get on if they had to apply for a rise in the same way as **Elizabeth Jane Addison**.

"Every year on our birthday, my sister and I had to write a formal letter to our father for an increase in our pocket money. If we made any spelling mistakes, a shilling was deducted from the new amount." I suspect that £7 would soon diminish!

Emily Fulker believed she had hit on a good way of persuading her two children to earn their pocket money. She gave them twopence a day with an extra penny for each day they made their own beds.

"At the end of the week my daughter got threepence a day but when I asked my son, 'How come you haven't made your bed?' he replied, 'I thought it worth a penny a day for you to make it for me'. I knew he'd go far!"

QUICK CROSSWORD 1

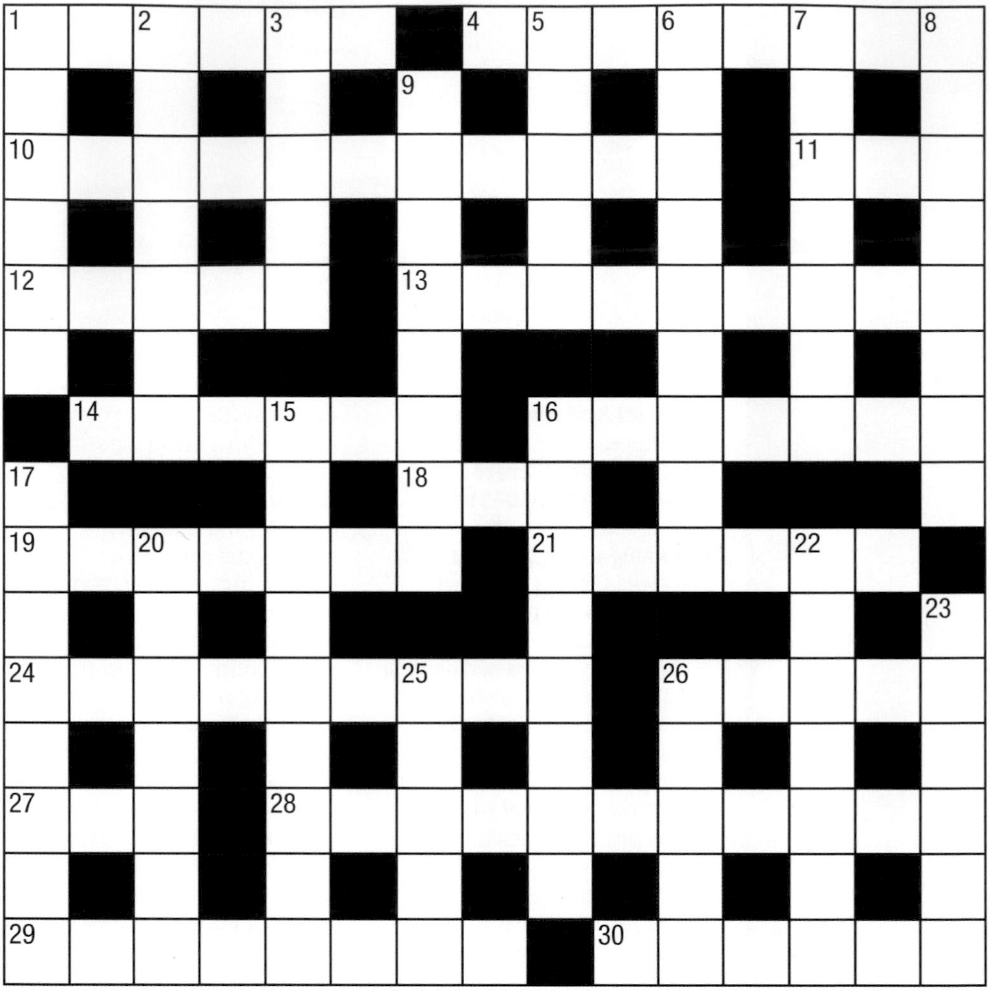

ACROSS

1 Recommence (6)
4 Seat of government in the Netherlands (3, 5)
10 MC at a formal meal (11)
11 Indication of a woman's original surname (3)
12 Painter's stand (5)
13 Track or field events (9)
14 Lady in distress? (6)
16 Sailing vessel such as Drake's Golden Hind (7)
18 Day before (3)
19 US drama series starring Glenn Close (7)
21 See 23D
24 Quarter of a city where Cantonese is spoken? (9)
26 Hawaiian farewell (5)
27 Secure with a rope (3)
28 Name adopted by Cassius Clay (8, 3)
29 Begrudged (8)
30 TV-filming room (6)

DOWN

1 Dastardly rogue (6)
2 Port in south Wales (7)
3 Roadside guesthouse (5)
5 Snag (5)
6 High jinks, tomfoolery (9)
7 Authentic (7)
8 Christian service of prayers also called vespers (8)
9 Irons, handcuffs (8)
15 The - - -, classic ghost story by Charles Dickens (6-3)
16 Famed Native American Apache leader (8)
17 Teacher (8)
20 Young ladies (7)
22 Panther (7)
23 & 21A Ian Fleming spy novel (6, 6)
25 Yellowy-brown shade (5)
26 Modify for new circumstances (5)

Puzzles

1 Which insects live in apiaries?

2 What was US President Joe Biden's former career?

3 Who wrote The Famous Five series of novels?

4 Which word follows: Peter, Pan and Point?

5 Who won Sports Personality of the Year 2020?

6 Which bird is also known as the sea parrot?

7 Goulash is a traditional stew in which country?

8 What is the smallest woodwind instrument?

9 Aviophobia is the fear of what?

10 In which English county is Leeds Castle located?

11 Which retailer became the sponsor of ITV's Coronation Street in 2021?

12 Glera grapes are used to make which wine?

13 May is the most popular month for weddings in the UK. True or false?

14 What is the national flower of France?

15 In which year were driving tests introduced in Britain?

Were you right? Turn to page 182 for the answers

A chance encounter

Unlucky in love Julie loses all hope when she's stood up, but does fate have other plans for her?

By George Hughes

The Sixth Form cloakroom was all abuzz as Julie and her fellow pupils at Queens High School bustled about, preparing to leave for home. It was the end of the school day and it being Friday, a welcome weekend lay ahead. The year was 1967 and The Beatles were top of the charts once again, their latest hit now being played from a small transistor radio a boy had secreted in his satchel. Julie's friend exclaimed,

"You must be looking forward to tomorrow Julie, a date with that hunk David!" Julie blushed – the swinging Sixties did seem to be passing her by, having had few dates. So she'd been surprised and thrilled when the good looking David invited her out to the cinema.

"Oh I am looking forward to it, but I'm not sure yet what to wear," said Julie.

"The shortest mini skirt you have!" exclaimed another voice.

"That will please David!"

Another girl's voice chimed in, "Sorry Julie but don't expect it to last long - he's had loads of girlfriends. He's gorgeous!"

Saturday afternoon eventually arrived for the excited Julie and she reached the cinema early for their 1.30pm date. She'd been to the hairdresser's that morning to get herself the latest fashionable beehive hairstyle. She was dressed very smartly too with her big sister's help,

dreams soon crumbled as the time of the date arrived and passed. She waited expectantly by the doorway, looking up and down the street, but by 2pm it was apparent that David was not coming - she'd been stood up!

It occurred to her now that perhaps he'd just been teasing her all the time and she began to feel rather foolish about it. Wiping tears of disappointment from her eyes, Julie glanced around as she left the cinema lobby and happened to catch a look of recognition from a boy stood outside alone. She knew that he was called Martin from her school but he was in the Upper Sixth form, a year older than her. She was somewhat embarrassed when he walked over to her, saying,

"Hi! I'm Martin... aren't you

> ## "Wiping tears from her eyes Julie glanced around and caught a look of recognition..."

from my school? Sorry I don't know your name."

"Hello Martin. Yes, I recognise you too! I'm Julie."

"Well Julie! Have you been stood up too? Makes two of us!" Julie, now further embarrassed, stuttered an excuse that her date was late arriving. When she mentioned who it was, Martin exclaimed, "I know David well unfortunately. I'm not surprised, to be honest, that's what he's like, sorry.

"My let-down isn't much of a surprise, actually. I've sensed for a while that my girlfriend's affections had cooled. Maybe by not turning up today it was her way of finally telling me!"

Julie made no comment but did feel sorry for the modest Martin, thinking that he was

quite handsome himself!

Just then it started to rain and Julie politely offered Martin shelter under her umbrella. They chatted for a minute before Martin exclaimed,

"Let's not totally waste the afternoon. Fancy joining me in the café along the street? At least we could enjoy a drink and play some records on the jukebox." After a slight hesitation, Julie stumbled a reply, "Yes, that would be nice."

Martin took Julie's arm as they walked along together beneath the umbrella, which gave Julie a tingle down her spine!

Reaching the café, they were soon facing one another over Coca Colas while the jukebox played the latest pop records. Becoming increasingly confident in his company, Julie chatted away warmly to Martin and, as they spoke, the pair discovered they had much in common.

Martin said coyly, "Well Julie, we're doing rather nicely for two date rejects aren't we?"

Julie went red remembering her forgotten date and she whispered, "I agree! Thank you for rescuing my day. You've been really kind!"

"Listen Julie. We're enjoying each other's company, so let's not let it end here in the cafe. Shall we go back to the cinema and try to make the film's second showing?"

Julie's head whirled, but she quickly replied, "Oh yes! That's a lovely idea. I'd love to."

Hours later after a great time together, as Julie's bus pulled off, she waved fondly to Martin. He had not only saved her failed date but they had just arranged to go to the disco together next weekend!

Julie sighed happily. Fate had made a chance encounter something so much more!

who had also given her a splash of her expensive love potion perfume!

Despite her very short skirt, her Mum complimented Julie on her appearance as she trotted off in her high heels to catch the bus into town.

Julie and her date were going to see the latest James Bond blockbuster movie, not that the actual film really figured in Julie's thoughts.

Sadly for Julie, however, her

Our crowning glory

*Writer Marion Clarke and **Yours** readers recall the grief we all endured to have curly hair*

I was either a slow learner or a hopeless optimist because I suffered several home perm disasters before I got the message that my fine, straight hair was never going to be miraculously transformed into the softly curling locks of my dreams.

Despite being named after Shirley Temple, **Shirley Balmforth's** crowning glory was as straight as mine, but her mum soon changed that. "She bought the dreaded packet containing a Twink perm. I had to sit for ages while my hair was sectioned and covered in tissue papers before being wound round the blue plastic curlers. Each curler was liberally dabbed with the lotion which had to stay on until the perm had set before it was rinsed off."

Charmaine Fletcher's mother was equally keen for her children to have gorgeous curls. "Even my brothers were subjected to Toddy Locks, a curling solution for babies, and I endured hideous perms from the age of seven.

"Later, I wanted a shaggy perm - a must for teenage girls in the Seventies. Alas, the hairdresser used insufficient solution - one side curled but the other didn't! Panicking, the hairdresser cut it shorter, saying it was too long to take the perm, but it looked worse. My mother bought me heated rollers to use on the offending side until it grew out."

Setting lotion was a vital step in the perming process - and one that could go horribly wrong, as **Pam Jones** discovered when she persuaded her mother to give her a home perm. "After she had applied the lotion, I lay across the bed

Blast From The Past

for the half hour as stated in the instructions. I had my head hanging over the side so the bowl on the floor would catch the drips. The next thing we knew, we'd both woken with a start and realised we had nodded off for two hours!

"It was panic stations as Mum tried to unwind what seemed like a hundred curlers welded tightly to my scalp while I screamed with pain and fright. I ended up with a head full of crinkly curls that no amount of washing would loosen. My lank hair has been a problem all my life, but no more perms for me."

A little white lie almost led to the end of a friendship for **Carole Hughes**. "In the Sixties, a friend asked me to give her a home perm. As she was blonde I asked her if she bleached her hair. She assured me that it was natural, but when I went to take the curlers out her hair was stuck like glue!

"She went home very upset and was late coming to work the next day as she had been to the hairdresser who had no alternative but to

Cheryl Whitehurst, pictured aged nine, very happy with her curly Twink perm!

cut her long hair close to her head. It looked awful! She then admitted that she regularly bleached it with neat peroxide! She forgave me eventually but it was an experience I'll never forget."

An experience **Elizabeth Hiddleston** will never forget happened when she was in hospital in the Fifties. When fellow patients decided to give her a PROM home perm after lights out, they were disturbed by the approach of the night sister. "We had to jump back into our beds - no time to rinse my hair. At breakfast, Sister Stewart made no comment about the plastic curlers I was still wearing. The only way to remove them was with

scissors. I was not a pretty sight."

When **Barbara Nuttall's** mum and her sisters experimented with Tweeny Twinks perms, her dad decided he didn't want to be left out. "So Mum did one for him. He was sitting with his curlers in when my auntie turned up unexpectedly. Dad ran into the kitchen and grabbed his cap. He sat there for three hours waiting for her to go home so that he could wash it off. Auntie kept asking, 'What's that smell?' although she never asked why he was wearing his cap. Needless to say, Dad just ended up with a head full of frizz, not curls!"

Who can forget the awful smell of the setting lotion? **Sue Marner**, who unwisely went to a party immediately after having a perm, likens it to rotten eggs and says: "I didn't have many friends that day!"

Mary Archer had a similar reaction when she was 14 and wanted to have curly hair. Her mother obliged by giving her a Pin-Up home perm. "What torture it was, but I persevered. I rushed off to the youth club where I joined my friends at the pool table. 'Heck, what is that dreadful smell?' said one of the boys and everyone looked at me. "No idea," I bravely lied. I never got to like that smell, but endured several more Pin-Up perms before I could afford a proper hairdresser."

But maybe there were worse things to endure in the name of beauty? **Jennifer Whittington** reckons so. "I think those who had home perms were very lucky. When I was little Mum used to put pipe cleaners in my hair and my sister's. We slept in them and in the morning we had curly hair, which we loved, but by lunchtime the curls had dropped out."

'What is he hiding?'

Mary suspects her husband is keeping something from her, but how will she react when the truth is revealed?

"I'm sorry, Mary, but I've checked with head office. You'll have to retire at Easter," said my boss of 12 years. "The rules have changed. It's policy."

I tried to argue, but it was useless. I'd been expecting to stay on for another year; now I only had six weeks left to work. I wasn't sure if I was scared or delighted.

Matters weren't helped when my husband didn't react the way I'd expected.

Jack's been working part-time since turning sixty, and was due to retire himself at Easter. When I tried to talk about the effect it would have on our lives, he changed the subject.

Immediately, alarm bells started ringing. You can't be married for 39 years and not know when your husband is hiding something from you.

For the first time ever, he'd made New Year resolutions and stuck to them. He was watching his weight and getting more exercise. What if he was having an affair?

That would explain why he was unhappy about me retiring early; if I was under his feet, it would cramp his style.

To clear my head I took our dog for a nice long walk. It was only when Buster started to slow down that I realised how long we'd been out. It was time to head home but when we got there, I could hear Jack talking to somebody on the phone. The moment I stepped into the living room, he hung up.

"Wrong number," he said, giving me a shrug.

I knew he wasn't telling the truth. Mysterious phone calls, watching his diet. They were all classic signs of an affair.

The next day, I made Jack's favourite apple pie for pudding. Normally Jack would polish it off and beg for a second helping but not this time –

By Linda Lewis

Short story

"I knew rather too much about Peter Bailey... he didn't have one roving eye, he had two. Spending time with Peter would put ideas in Jack's head"

he left half of it.

"It's really good but I'm not very hungry," he said. Then he dropped another bombshell. "I've decided to join the local gym. Peter Bailey's a member. He reckons it's a great way to meet people."

Unfortunately, I knew rather too much about Peter Bailey. He didn't have one roving eye, he had two. Spending time with Peter would put ideas into Jack's head - that's if they weren't there already.

That evening I called my big sister for some advice.

"You need to confront him," said Gill.

I knew she was right. I promised I'd speak to Jack after dinner the very next day.

I made one of his favourites: steak with fries and mushrooms followed by lime pie.

Unfortunately, Jack just picked at his food. "I ate something at work," he said.

"OK," I said. "What's going on?" I folded my arms and looked straight into his eyes. "You can't keep secrets from me."

His shoulders slumped as though he'd been deflated. "How did you find out?"

I wasn't sure how to reply, all I knew was that I needed to find out exactly what was going on, so I took a deep breath and braced myself for the truth. "Who is she?"

"What do you mean?"

'The woman who called last night. What's her name?'

"Samantha," Jack replied.

"Well you can tell Samantha to leave you alone. It's either that, or our marriage is over. I've had more than enough of this."

Jack stood there looking lost. "Are you saying you don't want to go away? I booked a walking holiday in the Lake District to celebrate us both retiring."

I didn't know what he was talking about. "You hate walking. You get tired taking Buster round the block."

"Yes, because I was so unfit. When you said you were retiring early, I panicked. I could see you leaving me behind."

"So that's why you joined the gym?"

He nodded. "I'm already feeling the benefit."

"OK," I said. "I still don't know who Samantha is."

"She's the travel agent. I asked her to pull some strings so we can take Buster with us."

"Then why did she hang up?"

Jack pulled me into his arms. "I wanted the holiday to be a surprise." He chuckled. "I never could keep secrets from you. No wonder I've never had an affair."

Luckily, I noticed the twinkle in his eyes and knew he was teasing.

"If you're suddenly so fit, put your trainers on. It's time for Buster's walk. Five miles OK?"

"Lead the way," he said.

As we set off, I was smiling. Retirement wasn't scary anymore, in fact I could hardly wait.

QUICK CROSSWORD 2

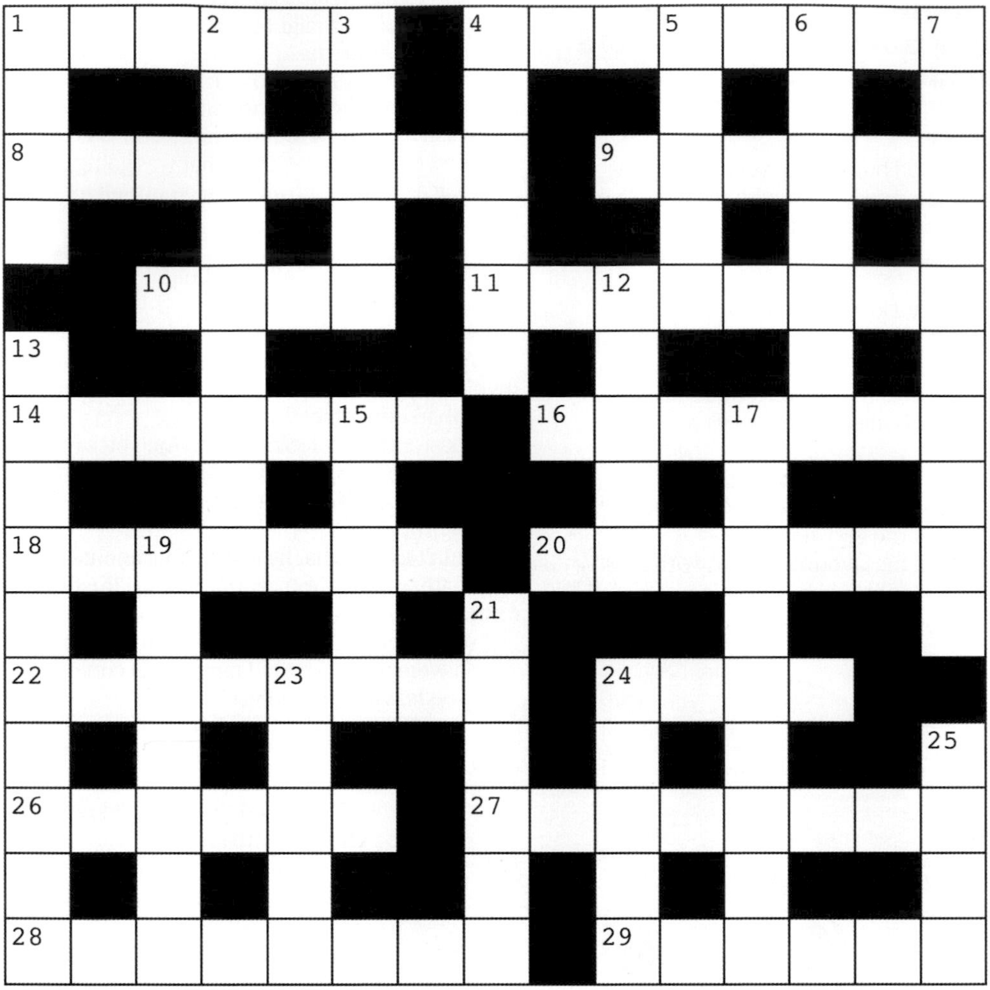

ACROSS
1 King's - - -, large amount of money (6)
4 Liquid-filled sleeping surface (5, 3)
8 Woman with dark tresses (8)
9 Sienna - - -, High-Rise actress (6)
10 Nervous, on edge (4)
11 Hannibal's birthplace (8)
14 Cultured, well-read (7)
16 Relating to fingers (7)
18 Poor management (7)
20 Flower arrangement (7)
22 Australian city (8)
24 Errand, job (4)
26 Pop - - -, Darling Buds of May patriarch (6)
27 Mount Kilimanjaro's country (8)
28 Fraudster (8)
29 Form of payment (6)

DOWN
1 Red gemstone (4)
2 Coastal city in Spain (9)
3 See 21D
4 Twist forcefully (6)
5 T S - - -, The Waste Land poet (5)
6 Northern Irish capital (7)
7 Indian leaf-growing town (10)
12 Elevate (5)
13 Pasta similar to spaghetti (10)
15 Roof worker (5)
17 Not having made a will (9)
19 Warm sheltered location (7)
21 & 3D Meek character who lives in a fantasy world (6, 5)
23 Outlets, egresses (5)
24 Long top worn in ancient Rome (5)
25 Travel charge (4)

QUIZ 2

1 Which couple won BBC's Strictly Come Dancing 2020?

2 Which word precedes: clip, cut and craft?

3 What type of creature is a sidewinder?

4 A Study in Scarlet is the first story about which fictional detective?

5 What is the official language of Brazil?

6 During which decade did Channel 5 start?

7 What is measured using the Beaufort Scale?

8 In which sport is the Stanley Cup awarded?

9 Which singers duetted in 2021 on Forever & Ever, Amen?

10 What is lapsang souchong?

11 Chocolate is the most popular ice-cream flavour in the UK. True or false?

12 Which river flows by Windsor Castle, Berkshire?

13 Which unit is used to measure horses?

14 Ricotta cheese originates from which country?

15 Who designed St Paul's Cathedral?

Were you right? Turn to page 182 for the answers

Little bird

When Kelly's solitude is disturbed she's forced to step out of her comfort zone

The thud against the window startled her and for a moment Kelly wondered whether she was being burgled. But as her heart settled into its usual rhythm she realised that something – perhaps a stone or a twig – had hit her living room window.

It was enough to draw her attention from the TV screen and encourage her to stand up and cross the room to peer through the blinds and see what had happened.

It was no mean feat, standing up. She'd been sitting a lot lately. Winter darkness had descended and she'd retreated into herself as she sometimes did, finding it hard to rally her limbs and get moving.

Recently, she'd even found it difficult to leave the house. Phone calls, except to their daughter Rachel, had become a struggle. The winter darkness had made everything close in and her fears had become monstrous and insurmountable.

From the outside, friends and family didn't notice much – she knew how to put on a performance when she needed

to. And working from home meant she didn't have to come face to face with anyone else very often.

But it was worse when she spent time alone: Tom had been working extra hours on site, as part of some special building project, he'd said. On the face of it, it was good news – it meant they'd have a bit more money and she could relax a bit.

"Maybe treat yourself," he'd said, looking at her kindly. "You could go to the shops?"

She'd looked back, wanting so much to be able to smile and please him.

"I'll try," she'd said "soon" and watched his face break into a smile.

Peeking through the blinds she saw that it wasn't a twig or a stone that had hit the window, but a tiny robin, which lay in the frost sprinkled flowerbed, its eyes closed, one wing folded, the other outstretched.

"Poor thing," she whispered.

It didn't seem right leaving it to lie there, even though there was clearly nothing that could be done. She couldn't bear the thought of its tiny body being carried off by the neighbour's

cat. Still, it was quite something to open the front door and step outside – it had been a few days since she'd last left the house.

Self-conscious of her unbrushed hair as she stepped across the threshold and onto the path, she glanced around her then darted to the little bird's body, her heart thundering. Removing her cardigan she covered the little broken creature and gathered it to her, before rushing back indoors.

It was light as a feather, and even through the thin knit of her black cardi she could feel that its body was still warm. She placed the bundle down on the kitchen table and was just about to search for a little shoebox to place it in when there was a movement – the arm of her

By Gillian Harvey

"She couldn't very well repair the wing, and putting the bird back seemed cruel"

cardigan twitched slightly.

Peeling back the temporary shroud, she saw the shine of a tiny black eye looking at her. The bird weakly raised its good wing and opened its beak as if to make a noise. It wasn't dead after all.

"Oh you poor thing," she said, wondering what could be done. She couldn't very well repair the wing, and the idea of putting it back outside in a bush or tree seemed cruel.

A computer search didn't reveal the answers she needed, but did yield a phone number.

Tentatively, looking at the little bird - its tiny heart still shivering in its chest - she dialled.

When Tom's car drew up outside, Kelly opened the front door and waited for him on the step. "How's the patient?" he asked her.

"Oh, she seems OK," she said. "I tried to make her as comfortable as possible."

"So it's a she?"

"No idea," she said. "She just seems like one."

Kelly carefully lifted the lid of the box, with its temporary holes, so he could see inside.

The robin flapped feebly and let out a tweet.

"Poor thing," Tom said. "Right, let's get going, I said I'd be back in an hour."

"Thanks for coming," she said, stepping outside for the

second time that day.

He didn't say anything, but she could feel Tom's surprise and relief as she got onto the car with him.

In the box on her lap, she could feel the robin hop.

"Do you think she'll be OK?" Tom asked as they drew up at the bird sanctuary.

"I'm certain," she replied. "This one's a real fighter."

"I'm sure she's very grateful to be rescued."

"Ha. Yes," she said, feeling a shiver of recognition.

Because although the bang on the window and the events that followed had been fleeting, the little bird had shown her that any moment life can change; and that even when everything seems lost, there is always hope.

Jelly on a plate

*Writer Marion Clarke and **Yours** readers remember the thrills and fun of children's parties*

Trampolines and soft play areas are great fun for today's children, but our parties had a special magic growing up in simpler times. Of course, some things don't change - parties will always be a great excuse for little girls to indulge their love of dressing up. I loved the blue angora bolero my mother knitted for me to wear over my pink taffeta party dress with a sash tied in a perfectly symmetrical bow at the back.

Doreen Parker also recalls a time when "mums who could sew made lovely long dresses with frills and sashes. We felt so special. We played Hide and Seek, Pass the Parcel, Musical Bumps and Sardines, and ate jelly and ice cream and paste sandwiches."

Food was as much of a highlight as the games were for **Heather Moulson**: "I won Pass the Parcel once, but the real treat for me was getting my hands on the pink blancmange that was always immaculately set from a mould. It still wobbled as it was put on your plate and tasted so wonderful."

Janice Chatten also had a sweet tooth - which proved to be her downfall! "As I gobbled down a sandwich and sausage roll, I kept eyeing the meringues, praying they would not be snapped up by the others before I had one. At last I was able to take a large pink one, oozing with cream. Blissfully, I sank my teeth into it. Oh horror! The inside was green mould and tasted revolting. I dared not say anything and had to force it down. It served me right for being greedy, I suppose!"

As parties were nearly always held at home, the number of guests was restricted - a consideration ignored by **Margaret Rymer** who was so thrilled by the prospect of her fifth birthday celebration that she

Blast From The Past

Jean Cooper sent this photo taken at a friend's eighth birthday party. Jean is in the front row, wearing a white dress, and the party girl is just behind her, proudly holding her iced cake.

invited everyone from school.

"I can still remember Mum and Dad's gasps of horror as children of all ages marched through the village towards our house. Thankfully, it was a sunny day so we could play outside. While we children were running around having fun, Dad had to rush off and buy more food."

At the other extreme was seven-year-old **Shirley Green** whose mother brought her and her brother up on her own. It was just after the War and money was in short supply. "I was allowed to invite only one

friend for my birthday tea and all we had to eat was fish-paste sandwiches and jelly with evaporated milk. Unfortunately, no birthday cake. Still, because we didn't know any better, we thought my party was delightful."

Pat Berkshire's party memories are also of the Forties: "But we still managed to give little gifts; hankies, soap or bath cubes for the girls, pencils and eraser sets for the boys. Sometimes the party girl or boy would get sweets from a saved sweet ration. Happy times, in spite of our dads being away in the services."

As well as preparing the party fare and a perfectly iced cake (no cheating with ready-made icing back then!) mums were expected to organise the fun and games as well. Fortunately for **Paula Buttifant** her mother had a flair for this. "My mum was fantastic at coming up with great ideas for parties and one in particular stands out. For my ninth birthday she drew a large spider's web on an old sheet and made a spider to go in the centre of it. Gifts for my friends to take home were stuck on the web.

"It was rolled up and put on the wooden airing rack above

the fireplace until my older sister, dressed as a witch and riding our cylinder vacuum cleaner, 'whooshed' into the room and unrolled it. Luckily, no friends were scared of spiders!"

But we all know that parties aren't always as jolly as they are made out to be, especially if you are shy by nature. **Christine Barrow** was an only child who led a sheltered life, a big disadvantage when invited to a party aged nine. "We all took part in a game in which we had to discover clues based on TV adverts. We had to guess what was being advertised, but as I was not allowed to watch much television (especially not ITV), none of them made any sense to me. I was really upset as I was the odd one out and felt so stupid." At one time or another, we've all been there, Christine!

When she was 11 and had just started going to grammar school, **Mary Archer** decided the time had come to move on from jelly, blancmange and Blind Man's Bluff. Her mother took Mary and two best friends out for afternoon tea. "We went to the Mandarin Tea Rooms in Staines. The tables were laid with pretty cups and saucers, shiny cutlery and fancy napkins. I ordered sandwiches, scones and cakes with a pot of tea. We giggled a lot and ate everything. Oh, how grown up we felt!"

Nessie

Will a trip to the famous Loch Ness reveal any sightings of the elusive monster?

By Ian Joynes

Visiting Loch Ness had long been on Sally's bucket list of things to do, and she was so excited when her husband, Peter, suggested they have a day out there, as part of their 30th wedding anniversary celebrations.

It was a long drive from their Scottish home, but they'd started out early, and the scenery along the way was simply delightful. Their misty start had turned into a gorgeous summer's day, as they pulled into the visitor centre car park at Urquhart Castle on the edge of the loch. Peter loved exploring ancient monuments, so this really was the perfect day out for them both.

"It's absolutely glorious here!" Sally beamed, as they got out to stretch their legs and took in the view of the loch.

"Wait a minute, put some of this on" she advised Peter, before squeezing from a tube of sun cream and applying it to the back of his neck as well as her own. "You know what happened last time we were out walking in the sun."

Peter smiled as he reminded himself how lucky he was to have Sally by his side to look after him.

Once inside, it was quite an adventure for both of them, imagining the lives of people that had inhabited the ruins, and there was the added bonus of trying to spot the mysterious Loch Ness Monster, though rather disappointingly she was nowhere to be seen today, no matter how hard their imaginations tried to find her.

"I'm sure that's something over there" Sally pointed excitedly, but Peter explained it was just the wake from one of the many cruise boats of tourists passing by.

They treated themselves to a cup of tea and a delicious slice of chocolate cake in the visitor centre café, before raiding the gift shop, and adding yet another tea towel and fridge magnet to their collection back home.

The afternoon was spent on board one of the vessels cruising the loch. Gordon, the captain, was the perfect host,

---

"Sally smiled and got to her feet before posing in front of three large rocks behind her"

---

explaining the history of the loch and some of its myths to all those on board. They even enjoyed a small dram of whisky each as part of the experience.

Their cruise lasted an hour, and was a beautiful way of spending the afternoon. The waters were quite calm once away from the other vessels, and they left a beautiful trail in the water as they cut through the tranquil waters.

The glass-bottomed boat was quite an experience, though the cloudy waters were not going to give up any of Nessie's secrets lightly today. She was nowhere to be seen.

Once back on shore they returned to the car and collected the picnic basket they had brought with them. It would serve as their tea before they began the long journey back home.

They followed one of the quieter nature trails across fields and through a small wooded area that left most of the other tourists behind.

Sally sighed as she held Peter's hand. There was nowhere more beautiful that she'd rather be right now, and she was proud to be with the man she'd married some 30 years ago and still loved dearly, even if he did have pale-white hairy legs and ill-fitting shorts.

They set down their picnic blanket near the shoreline and enjoyed some of Sally's home-made delights in the most tranquil of locations looking out across the loch. Sally's hampers were legendary among the family for being so well organised and prepared. Their fresh plate of sandwiches and flask of tea was the perfect way of ending their day out.

"Why don't I take one final photograph?" Peter suggested as they started packing away the hamper. "Go and stand next to those rocks over there."

Sally smiled and got to her feet before posing in front of the three large rocks next to the shoreline behind her.

"Cheese" she smiled as Peter clicked. It was another memory locked away for them to enjoy when they got back home.

Sally returned to where Peter was standing and grabbed the other end of the picnic basket he was holding before they turned and started making their way back.

Just then there was a loud splash in the water behind them. They both jumped, and turned around to where Sally had been posing moments earlier.

But there was no sign of the three large rocks she had been standing next to, just a very large ripple in the water...

QUICK CROSSWORD 3

ACROSS
1 Breed of hound (6)
4 Cunning person (8)
10 1415 battle (9)
11 Easy -----, Peter Fonda film (5)
12 Covered in powder (5)
13 Measure of intellectual development (6, 3)
14 Part, subdivision (6)
16 Wiltshire town (7)
18 Elevator operator (7)
20 Lacking friends (6)
23 Female religious leader (9)
25 Head of a monastery (5)
26 Code word for 'A' (5)
27 Inheritance tax (5, 4)
28 Aimed at (8)
29 Rubbed out (6)

DOWN
1 Alcohol distilled from wine (6)
2 Under discussion (2, 5)
3 Cagney & - - -, US TV series (5)
5 International airport in Bedfordshire (5)
6 Conan the - - -, 1982 adventure film (9)
7 Traditional card game (3, 4)
8 Military rank (8)
9 Trial course (5, 3)
15 Vacation home (9)
16 Company representative (8)
17 Animal that never forgets? (8)
19 Dolphin's limb (7)
21 Love's - - - Lost, Shakespeare play (7)
22 Resided temporarily (6)
24 - - - Redmayne, actor (5)
25 Tribe of Israel (5)

Puzzles

QUIZ 3

1 In which year in the Nineties was Netflix founded?

2 The Moon is oval shaped. True or false?

3 In which capital city were the 2020 Olympics to be held?

4 What does a soldier keep in a frog?

5 Nineteen Eighty-Four is which author's best-selling novel?

6 Erin and Harlequin are shades of which colour?

7 Which word follows: memory, river and food?

8 Which nuts are used in producing marzipan?

9 Who presents the BBC2 quiz Only Connect?

10 What is measured by a sphygmomanometer?

11 What do camels store in their humps?

12 Chevy Chase is a suburb of which American city?

13 What type of fruit is a Blenheim Orange?

14 In tennis, what is the term for 'zero points'?

15 What is an otter's home called?

Were you right? Turn to page 182 for the answers

Ralph's turn

When an act drops out of the village show unexpectedly, a farmhand shares his unique talent

By Steve Beresford

Yvonne peered out through a gap in the bundled curtains at the side of the stage.

Mallowdale Village Hall wasn't exactly a West End venue, but it was packed and everyone was thoroughly enjoying the show.

The applause and cheering for each act gave Yvonne the same funny feeling in her stomach that she felt on her wedding day.

This year's Annual Mallowdale Show was probably the best ever. And as director for the first time, Yvonne couldn't help but glow

with pride. There was a long way to go and a lot of people to keep organised.

She consulted her clipboard, tapping her pen down the list. "Alf, you're on next."

Alf, Mallowdale's 64-year-old Ed Sheeran lookalike, adjusted his wig and readied his guitar.

"And you're on." She jabbed her pen towards the stage and Alf strode out to the microphone like Freddie Mercury at LiveAid.

Every act so far was on top form and the show was whizzing along perfectly.

Well, almost perfectly.

"Yvonne! Problem!" Yelled Lisa Gaskill, assistant director. "Josie can't make it."

"What?!" Yvonne did not want to hear this.

Josie, the vicar's double-jointed, yoga-teaching wife, was scheduled to perform a display of highly technical contortionism.

"Impersonations by Mallowdale's answer to Johnny Morris weren't quite what she'd imagined"

"She says her stomach's in knots," Lisa said.

Yvonne frowned. "Isn't that what contortionists do?"

"From a dodgy curry last night."

"Oh. Ah." Yvonne grimaced. "But Josie's act is crucial."

The idea was that Josie would go on straight after The Asbo Hoodies and do her bodily twisting stage-front, with the curtain drawn behind her. Then The Asbo Hoodies - a teenage band playing Cliff Richard covers - could clear their instruments off and the scenery for the edited Romeo and Juliet performance could go on.

Yvonne had been training the sceneshifters and they were now like a Formula One pit stop crew - only two minutes and 26 seconds slower.

Without Josie's contortionism demonstration the audience would be sat with nothing to watch.

"So what do we do then?"

asked Lisa.

"What we do is find another act pronto to replace Josie. Any ideas?"

They both frowned. Then Lisa's face lit up. "How about Ralph?"

"Ralph?"

Ralph was a local farmhand. Yvonne wasn't aware the 19-year-old had any special talents – apart from knowing how to hotwire a tractor.

"Is he here?" she asked.

"I saw him arrive."

"And what can he do?"

"You know, voices. Whatsits. Impersonation things."

Yvonne wasn't exactly sure what that meant. "Is he any good?"

"He's brilliant!"

Yvonne thought about it. "Okay, fetch him. But be discreet. I don't want the audience realising anything's wrong."

Lisa returned backstage two minutes later with Ralph. Out of his mucky overalls and wellies and in casual trousers and a shirt he actually looked quite presentable.

"So, Ralph," Yvonne said, "Lisa tells me you do impersonations."

"Oh yeah!" He grinned.

"You any good?"

"Mates down the pub say I'm spot on."

"Fantastic."

"I can only do birds though."

"Oh." Yvonne stared at him. Wildlife impersonations by Mallowdale's answer to Johnny Morris weren't quite what she had been imagining.

She needed a demonstration, but with nerves starting to bubble the first bird she thought of wasn't exactly a common one in this area. "Puffin?"

"Well, I am a bit breathless." He'd arrived running. "Lisa said it were urgent, like."

"No, I meant..." Yvonne didn't know what a puffin sounded like anyway.

"Is he really good?" she asked Lisa.

Lisa nodded. "Trust me."

"Oh well. "Can you do three minutes?"

"Easy!"

"You're hired! You're on after the Hoodies. Lisa, get him ready."

"Will do."

Not long after the Asbo Hoodies were singing their last tune, Living Doll, and Lisa was ushering Ralph into position at the side of the stage, ready for his entrance.

"And... you're on!" Yvonne shoved him forward as the curtains closed and the sceneshifters began shifting scenery.

Ralph stumbled on stage to raucous applause.

"Hello, laydees and gennerman!" he announced, like a seasoned pro. "I'm here to perform my world-famous bird impersonations."

By now, Yvonne was thinking some gentle countryside culture might be preferable to the vicar's wife in a pink leotard inserting her toe in her ear.

Ralph struck a pose. "Here's one you'll all recognise. Ahem! Hiya, Sharon!" His voice was so shrill Yvonne winced in pain. "Yer new 'air looks ever so luvver-lee! That was the bird from the chip shop." He bowed. "And now the stunning blonde bird from the petrol station. Ahem! Pump number three, ain't it? Firty-free pounds."

Yvonne stared, horrified...

But Ralph was, astonishingly, actually really good. And the audience were in hysterics, instantly recognising all his impersonations.

And the potted Shakespeare went down a storm afterwards too. Especially as the – ahem! – stunning blonde bird from the petrol station was playing Juliet.

Santa's grotto

Writer Marion Clarke and **Yours** *readers recall the excitement of department stores at Christmas time*

During the festive season, department stores pulled out all the stops to make shopping an exciting experience, especially for their youngest customers...

Janice Baldwin writes: "Every year my Auntie Beryl took my sister and me to see Father Christmas at Derry & Tom's. We lived in Hounslow and went on the bus. We sat upstairs at the front so we could look at all the lights and always went to Trafalgar Square to see the Christmas tree from Norway. In store, we visited the café and ate Knickerbocker Glories. One year my sister ate two and was ill on the way home!"

Several readers, including **Mavis Moore**, treasured their early visits to one particular London store. "My father took me on the bus to Holborn to the biggest department store I had ever seen – Gamages! In the toy department, sales assistants demonstrated the mechanical toys. After a visit to Santa, we went to the counter where they sold Tom Smith crackers. I still remember the magic that was Gamages."

Marjorie Edwards was lucky enough to live only a sixpenny bus ride away from the much-loved Holborn store. "Ah! Gamages! I loved going there as a child. At Christmas, the queues to see Santa were so long they snaked right round the

Blast From The Past

Sue Rowley grew up in Tottenham, north London. "We had two small department stores nearby. The nearest one was called Rudd's and it had a toy department where my baby dolls were bought. My favourite store was Burgess's which had an X-ray machine to measure whether your shoes fitted. At Christmas, there was a roundabout in the store and you could visit Father Christmas. This is me doing just that in 1949. I don't look too happy, do I?"

We slowly made our way up each floor, getting more and more excited until we reached the top. We went through the grotto with its tableaux of fairies and elves until we were with Father Christmas who asked every child what they wanted before the elves passed you your gift."

Pat Rhodes went with her sister to Lewis's in Manchester where things were done a little differently. "We stood awe-inspired as Father Christmas climbed down a rope ladder from the store's famous dome. We followed him into his grotto where he gave out parcels from his big sack. My sister received a knitting set while I had a post office set."

Lewis's also had a store in Leeds where **Dorothy Brook** was taken with her brother and sister to see Santa. "My sister sat on his knee and when asked what she wanted for Christmas told him in a very loud voice, 'A pair of pink knickers'. My mother's face was a picture as she hastily pulled us all away.

Over in Edinburgh, **Elaine Gillespie** loved shopping trips to Goldbergs in Tollcross. "They had a rooftop café with caged parrots and other birds. At Christmas there was always a great display throughout the store. In Santa's grotto you could have your little one's photo taken sitting on Father Christmas's knee."

But young **Mervyn Law** didn't need Santa to make a visit to his local department store exciting. "My favourite was Featherstone's in Sittingbourne. I loved it when the assistant put the payment into a little pot on wires, then pulled a cord so the pot shot across the ceiling to Accounts, then came flying back with the receipt. I was lucky enough to be lifted up by the assistant so that I could pull the cord myself!"

shop. My very first doll, Pauline, came from there and I loved her blonde curly hair so much that I combed it to death! Eventually, she needed a wig and good old Gamages had just the thing, only it was long and straight and dark, but I still loved Pauline!"

It certainly wasn't dolls that attracted a youthful **Jim Connor** to the store's toy department. "Every year, in the run-up to Christmas, Gamages would exhibit, 'the largest model railway of its kind in the world'. For a budding enthusiast growing up in the Fifties it was an absolute must."

Readers who live in the north have equally joyous recollections of Lewis's department stores. **Olive Parry's** nearest branch was in Birmingham. "It was a great treat to see Father Christmas in his grotto. The queue wound all the way down the stairs and into the street.

Star struck

Will Linda's stars align to allow her to finally find love again?

FUTURE

By Alice Noon

Linda wished Madame Stella would hurry up. 'It's all in the Stars!' the pop-up ad on her Facebook page had proclaimed. 'Instant answers to your heart's desire!' What did Linda desire? A lovely new chap, that's what. It was six years since she'd lost Ron and while she'd loved him with all her heart, she didn't want to be alone forever. She had tentatively dipped a toe into the murky waters that were online dating but so far, no good. Linda instinctively felt fate needed to lend a hand. And that's where Madame Stella came in. The only thing was, that once Linda had revealed on the Zoom call that her star sign was Pisces, this so-called teller of fortunes had promptly fallen into a kind of trance.

Linda jumped as Madame Stella suddenly came to.

"There will be an instant attraction," she intoned, eyelids fluttering. "You'll recognise each other at once. You'll finish each other's sentences. You'll be soulmates. But you will have to do the running, Linda. Be bold, be brave! Make the first move! Take the bull by the horns!"

"He's Taurus, then?" asked Linda.

Madame Stella shook her head. "No, dear. A Pisces like you."

A fellow Piscean? Hmmmmm. . . Why then had 'Leo' flashed up in Linda's mind like a neon sign? 'Leo! Leo! Leo!' No matter what Madame Stella said, Amy's intuition was whispering, 'Leo.' She tried to shut it out.

"When will I meet him?" questioned Linda. "And where?"

"Very soon," Madame Stella smiled dreamily. "Today, in fact. As to where… think of your star

sign, dear. It's all in the stars!"

That evening Linda treated herself to a 'Blackbird' early bird special at the 'Twist of Lennon', the Fab Four-themed fish 'n' chip café in town. It was her first visit. As she tucked into her 'Getting Batter all the Time' meal deal, she came to the conclusion that Madame Stella must have made it all up. But then the door opened and in walked a man of about her age. He wasn't that tall, not that dark but definitely handsome. Linda's heart started to thump. It was him. She was sure it was. She watched as he walked up to the counter and heard him order the 'Plaices I Remember' special.

'Think of your star sign,' she remembered Madame Stella urging. Pisces… Of course! Maybe it was a tad cannibalistic but what 'batter' place for two Pisceans to meet than a fish 'n' chip shop? It all made sense. Trouble was, the neon sign in her head was flashing Leo again.

He came and sat down at the table next to Linda's, and flashed her a smile. What else had Madame Stella said? 'Be bold, be brave, make the first move, take the bull by the horns.'

There was an abandoned newspaper on the opposite side of her table. She reached for it and quickly found the 'Your Daily Stars' page. She looked across at him. He was looking right back at her.

"Shall I read your stars for you?" Linda blurted

"Pisces... today is the day for new beginnings. It's time to look to the future, go with your instincts and be spontaneous"

out. It was just about the boldest thing she'd ever done? "What's your star sign?"

'Leo, Leo, Leo,' flashed the neon in her mind.

"Er Pisces, actually," he replied.

Linda could hardly breathe. It was all coming true. Just as Madame Stella had predicted.

"Me too!" Her voice was a high-pitched squeak.

He smiled and put down his knife and fork. "Go on then," he said.

"Go on, what?" Linda couldn't take her eyes off him.

"The horoscope?" he laughed. "You were going to read it to me."

"Oh yes." She cleared her throat, willing the pesky 'Leo! Leo! Leo' neon to stop flashing. "Pisces - today is a day for new beginnings. It's time to look to the future, go with your instincts and be spontaneous."

"Sounds exciting," he said. "As it's for both of us, maybe we should act on it. Fancy a drink after this?"

An hour later, they were sitting in the pub next door, nattering away like they'd known each other for years. Just as Madame Stella had predicted, they were finishing each other's sentences. They could be soulmates, although given where they'd met and that they were both Pisces, perhaps 'sole' mates was more appropriate. But that neon sign continued to wink!

He walked her home and gently kissed her goodnight. Then, just as she knew he would, he asked to see her again. Linda was on cloud nine as she opened her front door. Then something suddenly struck her.

"Hey!" she called out as he walked away. "We don't even know each other's names. Mine's Linda. What's yours?"

The neon flashed brighter than ever. Linda laughed. Of course!

"No don't tell me, it's Leo, isn't it?"

He shook his head and smiled.

"Not nearly so posh as that. The name's Jim... Jim Lyons!"

QUICK CROSSWORD 4

ACROSS
5 Church minister (6)
8 Alcoholic drink taken to whet the appetite (8)
9 Coal miner (7)
10 Caesar, eg (5)
11 Objection (9)
13 Provided (with) (8)
14 Place of worship (6)
17 Urge (on) (3)
19 Noshed (3)
20 Amusement centre (6)
23 Lawless US frontier (4, 4)
26 Someone not in a relationship (9)
28 Topic, matter (5)
29 Charity fundraising event (4, 3)
30 Advocate, or position in football (8)
31 Tristan und - - -, opera (6)

DOWN
1 Woman's name, or Stephen King novel (6)
2 Jane - - -, star of Dr. Quinn, Medicine Woman (7)
3 Abducted (9)
4 Husband-to-be (6)
5 Likelihood, chance (8)
6 Latin American music (5)
7 Poisonous colourful evergreen (8)
12 - - - to Joy, poem used in Beethoven's Ninth Symphony (3)
15 Main performer (9)
16 Individual items (8)
18 Produce, conjure (8)
21 Brace, pair (3)
22 Coast, beach (7)
24 Certainly (6)
25 The Big Bang - - -, US sitcom (6)
27 Nikolai - - -, Russian novelist (5)

Puzzles

QUIZ 4

1 Which herbs do cats love?

2 What is the occupation of a Cordwainer?

3 A turophile is a lover of which dairy product?

4 Which word precedes: house, mug and surgeon?

5 Mageirocophobia is the fear of which culinary task?

6 In which sport might the participant assume the egg position?

7 Which planet is nearest to the Sun?

8 Which word means both a 'type' and 'caring'?

9 The ITV series McDonald & Dodds is set in which English city?

10 What is a butterfly's primary source of food?

11 Coconuts and dates grow on some varieties of which tree?

12 What is the title of the first Disney animated feature film?

13 What is a seascape?

14 Tomato ketchup was once believed to be medicinal. True or false?

15 What are baby squirrels called?

Were you right? Turn to page 182 for the answers

The end of summer

Everything is not as it seems when a couple decide to have tea on a windy cliff-top

By Liz Brewster

It was a windy day and as Emily looked out across the sandy grassy area that lead to the cliff top, she wondered if there'd be many customers in the snack bar today. If there weren't many there was a good chance she might finish and get home early for a change.

The summer holidays were over now so most of her customers would be a few stalwarts walking the cliff pathway, perhaps on their way to visit the old, now unused lighthouse. The area was known locally as 'The Stack' and in the height of the summer was a real tourist attraction.

A few windblown customers filtered in as the morning progressed and just after lunchtime an old lady who Emily didn't know wandered in

"Can I order tea for two?" she asked politely,

"And I hear you do excellent homemade cakes."

"Of course," smiled Emily pleased with the compliment. "Would you like to sit at the table in the window?"

The old lady hesitated and then said shyly "Would it be too much trouble to sit outside?"

"No of course not, there's a table just on the patio at the back."

"If you don't mind I would like to sit facing the sea, out there on the bench."

"Oh," said Emily trying to hide her surprise, after all not many people wanted to sit facing the Irish Sea even in the height of summer, let alone on a windy autumn day.

"Won't you be a bit cold?"

The old lady gave a little laugh. "No I'll be

"The old lady looked as if a puff of wind would blow her away. Why would she want to sit on a windy headland?"

for a friend and perhaps wanted to have a private conversation. Yes that must be it. And with that reassuring thought, Emily carried the laden tray out onto the grassy headland.

The afternoon passed pleasantly with just enough customers to keep her moderately busy. She glanced up once or twice and saw that the old lady had in fact been joined by a friend. From the back it looked like a man who at least looked better dressed for the weather in a sou'wester hat and a scarf. The old lady had also put a brightly coloured head scarf over her white hair. They seemed oblivious to their surroundings and deep in conversation. At 4.30pm Emily's friend Maggie breezed in.

"I'll have a quick cuppa and then help you wash up," she announced plonking down at one of the now empty tables. "Been busy?"

"Just steady, the usual and a few late holiday makers."

"Bit cold for the courting couple, I would have thought," said Maggie, nodding towards the bench on the headland.

"I know, I did try to dissuade her but she was adamant she wanted to be out there." Just as she spoke the door opened and as if on cue the old lady poked her head through it. "Thank you for the delicious tea, I'll be on my way, the light's starting to go."

"My pleasure," said Emily, "Hope we see you again."

"I hope so too," and Maggie and Emily watched her make her way somewhat unsteadily down the cliff path.

"Who was that?" said Maggie curiously.

"That was one half of your courting couple," smiled Emily.

"Don't be daft, the couple on the bench were just a couple of kids. Having a right old time they were, she was a right bonny lass and I'll tell you he was a bit of alright."

Emily stared at her astounded. "I'll just bring the tea things in," she managed to say at last as she headed for the door.

The bench still sat there, windswept and empty. Emily stared disbelievingly and as she stared she began to make out a faded and grimy plaque attached to one of the slats. Slowly she read...

"In memory of Giles Hunter Lighthouse Keeper.
He gave his life for this coast.
I am proud to have been his wife."

Emily bent to pick up the remains of the afternoon tea and a tear slid down her face as she saw that one half of it still remained.

fine, I'm used to it and I do love the view of the lighthouse".

"Well if you're sure."

"Yes I'm very sure," countered the old lady determinedly.

"Well then I'll bring it out to you." Emily could sense that there was no dissuading her. "You did say for two?"

"Yes please, two." And with that the old lady disappeared through the door.

Emily busied herself putting the tea together and pondering on the vagaries of people. The old lady looked as if a puff of wind would blow her away. Why she would want to sit on a cold bench, on a particularly windy headland was quite beyond her. And tea for two? She must be waiting

Thrills and spills

Yours *writer*
Marion Clarke and
Yours *readers share*
all the fun of the
fair and the circus!

The fair on Barry Island was the highlight when my cousin and I visited relatives who lived in the town. We could never decide whether to blow all our pocket money on a few rides like the big dipper or make our pennies go further by choosing the less exciting, but cheaper, attractions.

Christine Staff had the same dilemma. Her parents gave her half a crown to spend when John Thurston's travelling fair arrived once a year in Rushden: "This gave you five goes on the side stalls which included the coconut shy and hook-a-duck as these were

all sixpence each, but the big rides were one shilling. As we entered the fairground, we were greeted by the smell of onions

and sausages cooking. I used to stand and watch the lady making candyfloss and dipping apples into the toffee to make toffee apples."

Among the attractions that **Christine Young** and her brother enjoyed were hooking a duck to win a goldfish or an ornament made from chalk and going to see 'the tattooed lady'. And they weren't short of money afterwards: "When the fair was packing up to leave, we would mooch about the common to find sixpences and threepenny bits that people had dropped. If we came across a shilling, that was a real find!"

Blast From The Past

Sue Johnson got her money's worth when she and her friend had their fortune told: "As giggling 13-year-olds, we went to see the gypsy fortune-teller. She said my friend would marry a man with the initial G and I would marry one with the initial J. She's been a Griffith and I've been a Johnson for more than 40 years!"

Sharon Markham reminds us that fairs had a darker side: "It wasn't the toffee apples or the candy floss that drew me, but the sideshows: the tallest man in the world, the sheep with five legs and the woman in a bottle. There was even a boxing ring in which daring young men fought a kangaroo. These freak shows certainly wouldn't be allowed today."

But it was the jollier aspects that attracted **Edwina Jones**: "A highlight of my teenage years in the Sixties was to go to the Menai Bridge fair in Anglesey. My friends and I would walk there, about four miles each

BIG DIPPER

way, on a cold, dark and often wet autumn evening. It didn't put us off. We loved the noise, the music and the smells."

Julie Vinsome conjures up the atmosphere perfectly: "A frosty night, the smell of candyfloss and hot dogs. Bright lights and loud music. The screams from the ghost train and giggles from girls on the dodgems as the boys barged into them. I can still remember the thrill of The Whip and The Octopus rides and that faintly sick feeling afterwards. I didn't like the circus because I felt sorry for the animals and I'm frightened of clowns."

But for **Roger Hedges** it was a wonderful day when the circus came to his home town of Bromsgrove. "The circus arrived by the railway, but the recreation ground where it was to be set up was on the other side of town so the elephants, camels and horses walked there through the streets. Excited children accompanied the colourful procession."

Mrs M Nightingale says that when a circus arrived in Cambridge in 1958, it advertised for helpers to erect the tent: "My husband and I thought this would go towards our Christmas expenses so at 7pm off he went. Being six feet tall, he was one of the men chosen. After the tent was put up they had to queue for their payment

of a pound note. When he arrived home after midnight I couldn't stop laughing. He always said it was the hardest work and longest hours he'd ever done to earn one pound!"

A more risky fate awaited **Annmarie Lewis** when she and her small daughter had ringside seats at the circus: "One of the acts was a knife thrower. When no-one responded to his request for a volunteer, he came to where we were sitting and asked if I would do it.

"As he helped me into the ring, he said, 'Whatever you do, don't move an inch'. Up to this point, I'd thought the knives weren't real! I was placed in position by his glamorous assistant, then he threw the knives. Three on either side then, after a big drumroll, one just above my head. Oh, the relief when it was over!"

Doris Grimsley was living in Haydock during the war when she heard the circus was coming to the field behind their house: "My mother said I could go, but only if I collected manure for our garden. My friend came with me to the field and we put some large pats into our buckets and struggled back to throw the contents on the veg patch. Some days later I was told that it was elephant's manure that I had put on mother's runner-bean plants and it had burned them. But the bamboo support canes thrived!"

Time for a cat

Denise goes looking for a cat to keep her company but gets more than she bargained for

By Shane Telford

"You're just far too picky!" Amanda said to me, almost scolding. "Denise Collins, the hardest woman in the world to please."

"I'm not that bad." A blush so deep my cheeks felt on fire.

"What is it this time? Too short? Doesn't wear the right shoes? Supports Chelsea instead of Arsenal?"

"He just loves the ladies a bit too much... Honestly, his eyes were roaming the whole time we were having dinner."

And that was an understatement. Rob's attention was everywhere but me. Any time something in a skirt walked past his eyes lit up and he may as well have been dribbling into his glass of wine. The worst first date of my life, bar none.

"What about that other guy, the one who's keen on you?"

"Harry? No thanks..." I shuddered "A bit too keen... Psychological thriller keen."

"That's it then. You've run out of eligible bachelors." My best friend folded her arms "Time to invest in a cat. You'll need some company on those long, lonely nights."

"Don't be silly." I laughed nervously, not about to admit I'd already considered the idea.

I'd been scrolling aimlessly through Facebook when the advertisement appeared and piqued my interest. The local animal shelter was struggling to cope with all the rescue animals they'd recently taken in and were desperate for people to rehouse a pet or two. The picture they'd used had been the cutest ginger cat I'd ever seen, a real-life Garfield staring back at me with piercing eyes just asking to be adopted. I'd never been much of a cat person, but the picture had captured my heart within seconds.

"He's just the most beautiful thing I've ever laid eyes on." I peered down at the ginger ball of fluff and could feel my heart swelling by the second.

"Isn't he?" The man from the shelter sounded just as big a fan. "You can pet him if you want."

"Really?" A childlike excitement overcoming me.

"He's particularly fond of a scratch under the neck... but aren't we all!"

The more I stroked him, the more I could see myself doing it curled up on the sofa together.

"What's his name?" I asked, eyes not leaving his.

"Rascal. But I've no idea why... He's a saint compared to some of the animals we have in here... but then, they have been through a lot."

I was curious, so very tempted to ask about why Rascal was there in the first place, but I was already so in love with the little thing I knew it might be too much to bear. So instead, I just continued talking to the cat in that voice I have reserved for toddlers and adorable animals.

I was mid-coo when the first sneeze came, followed by another half a dozen.

"I think someone might be allergic..." The man beside me said.

My stomach tied itself into a knot at the suggestion. Before I could say I'd never been allergic to a cat before, another sneeze came, and this one was followed by itching skin. All those nights with Rascal curled up beside me were suddenly nothing more than a dream.

"I'm the same," the shelter worker admitted "If I don't take two anti-histamines before my shift I'm covered in hives! Come on, I've got a packet of them in the office."

I waved goodbye to Rascal and followed the man down the long corridor.

"It's a bit of a strange job to have if you're allergic." I said when he managed to find the tablets.

"Worth it though." Grinning

Short story

"I was mid-coo when the first sneeze came, followed by another half a dozen..."

"I get to see faces like Rascal's every day!"

I couldn't fault his logic.

"Probably not the best idea to live with him though. You'd be eating these for breakfast, lunch and dinner."

"No." A deflated sigh. "I got so fed up of my friend trying to find me a man to keep me company I thought a cat might do the trick instead."

"Oh, that old chestnut." If he was judging me it didn't show. Instead he just kept smiling.

"I don't suppose..." I heard my voice croak and wondered if it was the allergies or the nerves, either way I soldiered on, not quite sure what I was about to say next "you'd fancy a drink someday after work?"

"After work? Definitely not."

My heart sank for the second time that afternoon.

"Drinking on antihistamines? I'd be on my back after half a pint... The weekend might suit me better."

"Oh..." My eyes lit up, even if they were still itching.

I'd only known the man for 20 minutes, but I had a good feeling about this one. I mean, he couldn't be all that bad... not when he helps rehouse mistreated animals for a living, and risks an outbreak of hives just to do it. Now all I had to do was find out his name, or at least stop sneezing.

Puzzle answers

QUICK CROSSWORD NO. 1

Page 150
Across 1 Resume, 4 The Hague, 10 Toastmaster, 11 Née, 12 Easel, 13 Athletics, 14 Damsel, 16 Galleon, 18 Eve, 19 Damages, 21 Royale, 24 Chinatown, 26 Aloha, 27 Tie, 28 Muhammad Ali, 29 Resented, 30 Studio.
Down 1 Rotter, 2 Swansea, 3 Motel, 5 Hitch, 6 Horseplay, 7 Genuine, 8 Evensong, 9 Manacles, 15 Signalman, 16 Geronimo, 17 Educator, 20 Maidens, 22 Leopard, 23 Casino, 25 Ochre, 26 Adapt.

QUIZ NO.1

Page 151
1. Honey Bees; 2. Attorney; 3. Enid Blyton; 4. Out; 5. Lewis Hamilton; 6. Puffin; 7. Hungary; 8. Piccolo; 9. Flying; 10. Kent; 11. Argos; 12. Prosecco; 13. False – it's August; 14. Iris; 15. 1935.

QUICK CROSSWORD NO. 2

Page 158
Across 1 Ransom, 4 Water bed, 8 Brunette, 9 Miller, 10 Wary, 11 Carthage, 14 Erudite, 16 Digital, 18 Misrule, 20 Festoon, 22 Canberra, 24 Task, 26 Larkin, 27 Tanzania, 28 Imposter, 29 Cheque.
Down 1 Ruby, 2 Santander, 3 Mitty, 4 Wrench, 5 Eliot, 6 Belfast, 7 Darjeeling, 12 Raise, 13 Vermicelli, 15 Tiler, 17 Intestate, 19 Suntrap, 21 Walter, 23 Exits, 24 Tunic, 25 Fare.

QUIZ NO.2

Page 159
1. Bill Bailey & Oti Mabuse; 2. Paper; 3. Rattlesnake; 4. Sherlock Holmes; 5. Portuguese; 6. Nineties ('97); 7. Wind speed; 8. Ice Hockey; 9. Ronan Keating & Shania Twain; 10. Tea (Black); 11. False – it's vanilla; 12. Thames; 13. Hands; 14. Italy; 15. Sir Christopher Wren.

QUICK CROSSWORD NO. 3

Page 166
Across 1 Beagle, 4 Slyboots, 10 Agincourt, 11 Rider, 12 Dusty, 13 Mental age, 14 Sector, 16 Swindon, 18 Liftman, 20 Lonely, 23 Priestess, 25 Abbot, 26 Alpha, 27 Death duty, 28 Targeted, 29 Erased.
Down 1 Brandy, 2 At issue, 3 Lacey, 5 Luton, 6 Barbarian, 7 Old maid, 8 Sergeant, 9 Dummy run, 15 Timeshare, 16 Salesman, 17 Elephant, 19 Flipper, 21 Labours, 22 Stayed, 24 Eddie, 25 Asher.

QUIZ NO.3

Page 167
1. 1997; 2. True; 3. Tokyo; 4. A bayonet; 5. George Orwell; 6. Green; 7. Bank; 8. Almond; 9. Victoria Coren Mitchell; 10. Blood pressure; 11. Fat; 12. Washington DC; 13. Apple; 14. Love; 15. A Holt.

QUICK CROSSWORD NO. 4

Page 174
Across 5 Pastor, 8 Aperitif, 9 Collier, 10 Roman, 11 Complaint, 13 Equipped, 14 Chapel, 17 Egg, 19 Ate, 20 Arcade, 23 Wild West, 26 Singleton, 28 Issue, 29 Flag day, 30 Defender, 31 Isolde.
Down 1 Carrie, 2 Seymour, 3 Kidnapped, 4 Fiancé, 5 Prospect, 6 Salsa, 7 Oleander, 12 Ode, 15 Headliner, 16 Articles, 18 Generate, 21 Two, 22 Seaside, 24 Indeed, 25 Theory, 27 Gogol.

QUIZ NO.4

Page 175
1. Catnip or catmint; 2. Shoemaker; 3. Cheese; 4. Tree; 5. Cooking food; 6. Skiing; 7. Mercury; 8. Kind; 9. Bath; 10. Nectar; 11. Palm Trees; 12. Snow White & the Seven Dwarfs; 13. A photo or painting of the sea; 14. True; 15. Kittens.